CONTENTS

Editorial

In Paris in the Autumn of 1989 three Muslim girls, observing their own religious custom, went to their school wearing Muslim headscarves. The ensuing political storm, which continued unabated into 1990, has brought back sharply into focus one of the fundamental questions related to Western democracy: the nature of the relationship between religion and the state. The 'scarves affair' was primarily a dispute between practitioners of Islam and the secular state. The controversy in France and similar recent controversies elsewhere, however, have forced a general and, for many, radical reappraisal of the wide and complex issue of religion and its relation to politics. This issue of *Contemporary European Affairs* is a contribution to the debate.

Bruno Etienne starts with a discussion of the Muslim communities in Europe: a difficult task as there are no European-wide figures on religion. Harry Goulbourne and Danièle Joly offer an overview of the Asian and Caribbean minorities in Britain and an examination of these minorities from the religious perspective. Other articles on the current debate are those by Gianni Bozzo, Hamit Bozarslan, and Georges Corm. Gianni Bozzo looks at the way in which the Christian religions have coexisted with the secular state, examines the 'return to religion' and contrasts these traditions with the Islamic. He argues that the future of the world will depend now to a large extent upon the choices made by the Islamic community. Hamit Bozarslan looks at Turkish Islam in the Federal Republic of Germany. Turkey, as the principal source of immigrant labour in Germany, could be said to be a part of the European Community in that respect. Georges Corm looks at the Middle East where the religious clash seems to surface with the most vigour, although he argues that the quarrel is not specifically about religion and that an interpretation of the problem as a fundamentally religious one impedes a proper solution (and, Corm argues, there is now the possibility of a solution given the waning of super-power influence).

Edgard Pisani notes the continuing and growing existence of large Muslim minorities in Europe, and argues that there is a way forward through the development of respect for the Islamic religion by Europe and the acceptance by the Muslim minorities of the secular state. This 'European' solution implies a secularization of the British state as well. Etienne concludes that the different Muslim communities tend to be grouped by nationality and that there is no standard statute for Muslims in Europe (most of them immigrant workers), something that will have consequences after 1992 and the free internal European labour market.

Also in the issue are articles by Penny Lernoux, who looks at Papal influence through Opus Dei in Central and South America, and by Renée Fregosi who discusses secular and politico-religious interaction in Europe in its long term historical context.

This issue contains, in addition to the section on politics and religion, the European Dossier which contains a discussion by André-Gwenaël Pors of the difficulties hospitals will face after 1992 and in particular the need for a European approach to health care. Although health is not mentioned in the European Treaties the inevitable spillover effects of economic integration will, the author argues, lead to initiatives in this field. There are also the usual Literary section (in this issue a contribution from the German peace campaigner and author Siegfried Lenz), the section 'Europe Now' which is an interview with the new president of the European Parliament, Enrique Barón, and the reviews section which looks at two books which deal with topics of particular importance to Europe at the present time: Eastern European Cinema and the cultural reality of Europe's regions, in this case the Campos de Nijar in Southern Spain.

D S Bell and J Gaffney

Politics and Religion

The Secular State

Edgard Pisani

It is possible for an agnostic to respect religious beliefs and believers. Is it possible, however, for a believer to respect other beliefs and non-believers?

Do believers wish to spread their beliefs and extend such activity beyond their private lives to all aspects of public life? Would we all fight in our societies and in the world at large to defend our right to believe or not to believe? These several questions now confront many countries.

Fundamentally, a secular political system is one that defends all religious and non-religious beliefs, all philosophical and ethical beliefs. The secular state preaches and defends reciprocal tolerance. It forbids any group whether of believers or agnostics (and whether it forms a majority or not) to claim power and to use it to assert the spread of its beliefs and its own domination. In practice, in the historical struggle of the secular state its supporters have often become its committed activists, that is to say, that going beyond their struggle for the secularization of the state and the division of religion and politics, the secularists have denied God. The secular state, and France is a case in point, has thus run the risk of altering its own principles and compromising its own gains, given that God's children cannot but react against the concerted action of the godless.

There is, therefore—and let us restrict ourselves here to Europe and to the Christian religions—a relationship between the Reformation, the Declaration of the Rights of Man, and the confrontation that took place at the beginning of the twentieth century, in France and elsewhere, at the time of the separation of Church and State.

The Reformation was a long struggle against the clergy's claim to be the privileged mediators between the Creator and his creations, and against the Church's attempt to introduce into both thought and practice its sway over temporal power. This attempt, bringing it in line with other political sovereignties, in fact threatened to restrict its influence to those areas it controlled by military force. The Reformation was also a struggle against the values that had been encouraged by secularization, a struggle against licence and indulgence, and a search for original virtues.

Rome's failure to draw the lessons from such warnings meant that the Schism was bound to happen. This important epoch (whose historical importance is often not properly appreciated) saw the rebellion of God's children or, rather, of the clerics, against the authority of the Church. Centuries later, the discrete but merciless debates surrounding the message of Vatican II have recreated the age-old divisions. In all of these quarrels there is barely any questioning of belief itself, at least from the point of view of the outside observer. The debates do not concern metaphysics, the nature of the cosmos, nor values; only religious practice, hierarchy, authority, power, and the role of the clergy *vis-à-vis* God on the one hand and the people of God on the other.

Just as serious in many respects is the major struggle which took place two centuries ago and whose quintessential act was the Declaration of the Rights of Man and the Citizen. Here, it was not a question of practices and hïerarchies but of the founding principles of Law. It involved replacing divine law with human law and Revelation with rational enquiry: the human being became no longer the mere object of law but both its subject and object, the maker of the rules whose responsibility and constraints he accepts, along with the ability to change the rules according to accepted procedures. Law became no longer the expression of divine will whose only interpreters were the king and the Church, but the expression of the will of the people. The people intended—without precluding recourse to transcen-

dent values—to define its own values, rules, structures, practices, and sanctions. Today, still dazzled by the political and
military events of the French Revolution, we have not given this
historic break its due credit. In August 1789 there was a change
in the nature of legitimacy. Like before, refusing to draw the
lesson of the Enlightenment and the long and arduous work of
the legists, the new 'legitimists' refused to take into account the
claims of the people of God. They wanted a society 'without
God', even though at the beginning it was only a question of
freeing the political from the religious and of leaving to the
citizen the care of sorting out by himself the affairs of the century.

In France, the separation of Church and State at the beginning
of the twentieth century was a new episode in the struggle for
legitimacy. The confrontation began in the 1870s at the moment
of the attempt to restore the monarchy after the defeat of Napo-
leon III at Sedan.

The new Republic immediately found itself faced with the
combined forces of the civil and religious legitimists who sought
to put back on the throne a sovereign who owed nothing to
popular sovereignty, and whose authority was to be based upon
divine right. The attitude of the legitimists meant that the
struggle for the Republic and against the pretender was seen as
a struggle against the Church, and soon after a struggle against
religion itself. It was in these circumstances that the education
question arose.

It grew out of the deliberately erroneous interpretation of the
political intentions of the creators of state schools. Doubtless,
these latter needed to stop the schools run by ecclesiastics from
becoming the breeding ground for the legitimists' 'battalions',
but this was not their main concern. They believed that education was the basis of a society in charge of itself and that universal
suffrage (until very recently the suffrage had been based upon
property) called for an education system that was also universal.
However, for there to be education for all, two principles had
to be established: education had to be compulsory and,
therefore, free. Given, however, that education was compulsory
it also had to be secular, that is to say, as Jules Ferry said in his

Lettre aux Instituteurs 'respectful of a child's soul':[1] neutral, open, and not in conflict with the teachings of the family, nor with those of religion.

The struggle for political power, in which the Church was not a neutral observer, led to further developments. Although Catholics henceforth accepted the situation, a situation which respected their beliefs, many serious divisions—which took nearly a century to overcome—could have been avoided (not that all of them have been resolved today).

In this way, in this third historical phase, it was at the level of the foundation of the legitimacy of political power that the problem lay; religion as belief, as interpretation of the universe, as philosophy and as ethics was only involved in the conflict to the extent that those who considered themselves its protectors and those who wished to profit from the political and social system based upon it consciously intended it so. The conservative right used religion in order to maintain the system it wanted.

In a word, the secular issue is not a recent one. Nor is it linked only to the events we are describing here. It is an integral part of our civilization borne of a thousand years of history and a myriad of conflicts: the Crusade against the Cathares, the Saint Bartholemew's Day massacre of 1572, the Dragonnade persecutions, the Edict of Nantes, and the revocation of the Edict of Nantes. The belief in the secular state is not the result of a decadence which saw the decline and loss of fundamental values, especially spiritual ones, but a struggle which has left its mark on history. Today's secular spirit is not a secularism by default, but the fruit of experience, a compromise we believe in, and which is based upon very demanding social, and deeply human, values.

From these many trials, from what we can legitimately call a collective quest, came a society where religious tolerance became established even before political tolerance and where the overwhelming majority of men and women believe that each person's

---

[1] Jules Ferry, French Prime Minister and Minister for State Education for much of the period 1879–1885; regarded as the architect of the French secular education system.

liberty should be respected, and that personal beliefs and political choice are independent from one another. This, of course, brings with it many problems.

This reciprocal autonomy of politics and ethics *vis-à-vis* religion characterizes our society. And it cannot be otherwise. Once individuals, as citizens, are responsible for the political choices of the Nation, it becomes dangerous for religion itself to be subject to the inevitable changes wrought in the political sphere. For religion to be respected in the context of the contradictions of political choices, it must itself remain politically neutral. In order to avoid becoming the site of confrontations in which religion plays a decisive role, politics itself should also remain neutral as far as religion is concerned. Doubtless there is something perhaps over-optimistic in this balanced idea of national life but it is precisely this which has fashioned our modern history. In this way, in differing degrees in the various European countries, this growing convergence is one of the most significant phenomena in the development of this part of the world.

Today, many people have the feeling that this balance is being threatened as a result of what is essentially a Muslim immigrant community. We should not forget that Catholic immigration from Italy, Spain, and Portugal also provoked strong reactions, but it cannot be denied that the Muslim immigrants, more numerous before, in fact, than now, are perceived as a threat to indigenous workers threatened by unemployment. And the view prevails today that immigration should be combated because the immigrants subscribe to a religion that is not our own, that 'assimilation' is impossible because they are Muslims.

There is something very strange in this view which is more a political one than a religious one. It is the people who are themselves both monotheistic and fundamentalist, and who call for a return to ancient principles, who are the most vigorous opponents of the immigrant Muslim monotheists. They build into a religious conflict what can and should be seen as a problem of coexistence between a national majority which bases itself on the distinction between the religious, the moral, the social, and the political, and a minority of 'newcomers' who believe in a system where religion creates, explains, and contains everything.

The problem must be clearly stated, and this free from all the tensions that arise from the differences in language, habits, and behaviour, and from the social marginalization which is the inevitable result. And we must state it while remaining true to ourselves and respectful of those we have welcomed among us.

This is not a minor question: there are in France more than twice as many Muslims than there are Jews and Protestants put together. In Germany there is now a Turkish 'colony' which is growing all the time. The British inner-cities are host to many Indians and Pakistanis. Italy and Spain, until recently impenetrable because of their demographic growth, now welcome Algerians and Moroccans. This is not a passing crisis: the demographic disequilibrium and the high birth rate of the immigrant communities suggest that the number of Arab, Turkish, and African Muslims will double in ten or fifteen years time. The problem will not solve itself. It is true that France, for example, has been a remarkable melting pot throughout its history. Today, however, given the numbers of immigrants, the lack of attention paid to what this means for the education system, the creation of homogeneous ghettos of migrants, and the ties they keep with their mother country, mean that the Arab and Muslim community pose a new problem and one which will not be solved by ignoring it.

We will not here analyse the educational problem, nor those of employment, housing, social integration, nor the fact that there is a significant gulf between the according of French citizenship and French society's views concerning such conferring of citizenship. Here we shall examine only the religious aspect.

In France there are several religions, and several Churches, as well as communities and families of thought who do not claim any religious affiliation. After many historical developments, they all benefit from freedom of worship which is guaranteed by the protection of a neutral state. This balance is confirmed by a reciprocal tolerance and one which allow the preaching of beliefs. The political system itself proclaims and guarantees respect for other beliefs. There is, therefore, respect at both the personal and the institutional level. Our system accepts diversity, accepts 'the other' and his or her differences.

What place does Islam intend to take in such a society? What position does it intend to take *vis-à-vis* this political philosophy which recognizes religion without giving religious leaders institutional or political responsibility? We can envisage two positions, one of which must be chosen, and which rests as much upon the choice of Muslims as upon that of the state.

The first is for Islam to accept purely and simply the prevailing political philosophy and to become part of that society whose rules it accepts and in which it has the guaranteed right to preach its faith. One would be, say, a French Muslim, just as are the Jew, the Catholic and the Protestant. This seems to have been the choice of Muslims who have been in the country for a long time who do not wish to abandon their roots nor cut themselves off from society.

The second position is to claim the advantages, benefits and guarantees of society while claiming the right to practise intolerance. This position leads directly to a spirit of conquest which will lead to the rejection of Muslims by society.

The Muslims living in Western Europe, and the Muslim communities which have organized themselves and developed have no other choice. Their religion thrives in a secular society which guarantees them the same rights and requires the same duties as others. Tolerance breeds respect; intolerance breeds rejection.

We should be careful here not to over-dramatize the situation. Many of the street demonstrations of 1989 were of little significance. In general, Muslims wish to remain what they are in a society whose organizing principles they cannot change. The problem, in fact, lies elsewhere. It lies in the Muslim countries themselves, where Islam holds either complete or hegemonic sway. In these countries religion, ethics and politics are one. Only those who respect the word of the Prophet belong to the community.

The problem is not the same in all Muslim countries, nor the same at different moments in the recent history of Islam.

Generally speaking, the struggles by Arab nationalists for the independence of their countries were based less on a religious claim than on a national one. It was only with the passing years that the dissatisfaction of the masses (provoked by the mistakes or inefficiency of their governments) created the fundamentalist momentum. This momentum has often been encouraged by the masses' disillusioned with the political game, by the difficulties of daily life, but also by the irresponsible behaviour of both the East and the West. The masses sought the answer to their suffering in religion. Sometimes it has been the lack of democracy in the secular Arab states which has provoked the politico-religious outburst. In this search for identity the various countries have not achieved the same equilibrium, nor experienced the same tensions. Overall, however, seen from the North, the Arab countries all run similar risks of radicalization. Confusing internal and external politics, many European observers see a threat to the stability of the whole region which goes from the Gulf to the Atlantic.

If we are not extremely careful, one day dangerous tensions will develop around the Mediterranean between two human groups who will either have to accept each other in a positive manner or else fight. Europe must demonstrate its respect for Islam and ensure that others respect its own civilization so painfully built over the course of its long history. Muslims must renounce their desire to modify societies in which they are in a minority from the moment that such societies guarantee them the same rights that they guarantee to all other beliefs and non-beliefs.

*   *   *

Wars of religion or secular state, wars of religion or mutual respect between states in a secular vision of the world. Those are the choices. The secular state does not deny the sacred. It ensures that those who subscribe to it cannot govern the diversity of society in its name. For André Latreille, the secular is the juridical expression of the freedom to make an act of faith, and to refuse all faiths. The secular state does not call for non-belief, it wishes only that the believer and the non-believer are accorded the same respect; both live within it respectful of the law which is its essential expression. Is the problem so simple?

Are there those who believe and because of this belong to a religion and those who do not and lay claim only to reason? Is the essential debate between the religious and the sacred on the one hand, and the rational and denial of the sacred on the other?

There are among secular people themselves, more than we realize, women and men who are sensitive to and show respect for the sacred, who are involved in a perpetual search for the sacred, yet who, nevertheless, do not accept the authority of revelation nor that of institutionalized religion. Perhaps it is simply part of human nature that we have somewhere within ourselves a secret knowledge of the sacred, an implicit certainty of an immanent reality.

There are what we might call authentic non-believers, whose reference is humanity alone. But here too we can see that such people wish desperately to believe in Man and men's capacity for perpetual transcendence; a transcendence which is all the more heroic because it is based upon no certainty. And this search itself leads to the sacred because, as Roger Caillois has put it, the sacred is the being, the thing or the idea which governs men's conduct, that which for him is not negotiable, must not be abused or ridiculed, that which he will neither deny nor betray at any price.

The secular state is the only state that can ensure for both the individual and the community the free choice of life's meaning. It is the guarantee for every person that they may enter into a free relationship with the sacred.

The secular spirit abandons its own definition when it refuses to take the sacred into account; when it transforms the rule into an end in itself. Wherever there is diversity—and where is there not?—the secular is the only guarantee of the free enquiry of the mind, and, therefore, of its responsibility.

From the Secular† to the Politico-Religious: Reflections on *The Name of the Rose*

*Renée Fregosi**

> A product of modern European
> civilisation, studying any problem of
> universal history, is bound to ask himself to
> what combination of circumstances the fact
> should be attributed that in Western
> civilisation, and in Western civilisation
> only, cultural phenomena have appeared
> which (as we like to think) lie in a line of
> development having *universal* significance
> and value.
> Max Weber, Introduction to *The
> Protestant Ethic and the Spirit of Capitalism*

For some years now we have been seeing in Europe a revival of interest in things medieval. This 'vogue' for the Middle Ages has been expressed intellectually and commercially, in both philosophy and its imitations, and in the theatre and in the media. The reissue or publication in paperback form of works hitherto reserved for the specialists are also indications that the Middle Ages is 'selling well'. Many television programmes are devoted to the period, and even fashion has recently adopted the medieval 'look'.

In terms of the revival of interest in the Middle Ages, the

---

* Director of the French Socialist Party's Research Institute (ISER)

† The French word *laïque* cannot be properly rendered into English as it carries within it, largely because of politico-historical developments in France, a far more positive connotation and the implication of a political project that affects all political and social institutions.

success of Umberto Eco's *The Name of the Rose* is exemplary.[1]
A 'difficult' book (it has a very particular rhythm, a Borgesian
style, contains complex theological and philosophical debates,
and an equally complex crime novel plot; and it is, moreover, a
very long book), it has, nevertheless, been well received by a
very wide public. Even though the book is not always read cover
to cover, it has sold thousands of copies, and it is clear that the
'model reader' that Eco visualizes as he writes has been joined
by a host of what he has called 'empirical readers'.[2] This unexpected popularity has, in fact, caused the author himself to try
to explain the phenomenon. In his *Postscript to the Name of the
Rose*, Umberto Eco gives what are essentially stylistic explanations to make 'the novel readable for unsophisticated
readers',[3] that is, for people who do not normally like such
'cultivated'[4] literature. To Eco's explanations we must also add
both the talent of the author and his knowledge of the Middle
Ages.

   These are not, however, the only reasons for the book's success. Umberto Eco himself puts forward another reason: the
Middle Ages tells us about the present period—even though he
seems to dismiss this as a relatively trivial point, 'it is no use
saying that all the problems of modern Europe took the shape
in which we still feel them during the Middle Ages: communal
democracy and the banking economy, national monarchies and
urban life, the new technologies and rebellions of the poor'.[5]
However, he feels that because we also usually think of the
Middle Ages in what we might call a Knights of the Round Table
way, that is, in the received commercial and somewhat glitzy
style, the general appeal of the large medieval frescoes cannot
really explain the success of a book dealing with that other Middle Ages of clerics, weighty tomes, and theology.

   Should we not rather see the Hollywood-style depiction and

[1] Eco, U., *The Name of the Rose* (London, Picador, 1984).
[2] *Postscript to The Name of the Rose* (New York, Harcourt Brace Jovan-
ovich Publishers, 1983) p. 50.
[3] Ibid. p. 34.
[4] Ibid. p. 39.
[5] Ibid. p. 73–74.

the scholarly work as being not mutually exclusive but in fact as two aspects of the same process, a process which highlights both frivolity and seriousness, both the philosophy and the daily life of the Middle Ages? Of course, qualitative differences remain. A film such as *Excalibur*, and, to a certain extent, the film based on Eco's own novel, give the public what it wants, that is to say, a stereotype of the Middle Ages, whereas the book *The Name of the Rose* shows to its readers what they should want 'even if they did not know it'.[1] However, the 'demand' for the medieval that we are witnessing today does not come from nostalgia alone. This could easily just simply take the form of traditional neo-romanticism, or what Eco calls amnesia. For Eco, 'the Middle Ages are our infancy, to which we must always return'.[2]

The conscious and unconscious demand, the multi-faceted interest in the Middle Ages are, in fact, the result of a search for a foundation, for explanatory models, for reference points, and for a way of building 'a new reality': the nostalgic vogue for the Middle Ages is, in fact, an indication of the fundamental importance of the Middle Ages for contemporary Europe, a Europe once again in search of its true identity. The Middle Ages was both a historical and a fantasy period which saw the emergence of a geo-political reality as well as a social and cultural area which accepted (while at the same time breaking down) the ancient line dividing the Orient from the Occident, and saw the emergence, both by means of and in opposition to Christian universalism, of the nation states.

It is true that what is usually called the Middle Ages is a very long period, more than a thousand years, in fact, from the fourth to the fifteenth century, and subsumes realities that were very different from one another both in terms of social organization, and culture, and cultural developments.

The popular view, in France at least, tends to telescope the Carolingian Renaissance, the legendary figure of Saint Louis handing out justice under his oak tree, and the epic Hundred Years War, punctuated by Joan of Arc's herioc resistance. It is

[1] Ibid. p. 50.
[2] Ibid. p. 74.

in part a jumble of school history lessons, in part a consciousness of national origins whose roots are both Roman and Frankish, and which draws upon Christian culture and the anticlericalism of the fabliaux. Empires, feudal systems, and statist monarchies succeeded one another, interacted and fused with one another over this long medieval period of population movements and wars, a period which saw languages mixed together and new ones created, and philosophy and thought develop in response to the myriad of often opposing influences upon it.

The present vogue for the Middle Ages, of course, conjures up pell-mell various different periods and brings them together into a kind of mythical and aesthetic reference point. And, in a certain way, although each historical phase both resulted from and broke with the preceding one, the Middle Ages does present a complex and contradictory unity and a very real coherence. It is difficult to identify precisely the emergence of that form of social organization known as the state and, in particular, that form of it which seems to be a specifically Western phenomenon: the nation state. However, for the purposes of our discussion, let us concentrate on the last four centuries of the Middle Ages, from the twelfth to the fifteenth centuries, and, in particular, on the structural complexity of the thirteenth and fourteenth centuries in Europe. To be even more precise, over and above the many historical references and the elaboration of the myth, today's interest in the Middle Ages draws essentially upon that period in Europe between 1204, the sacking of Constantinople during the Fourth Crusade, and 1492, the discovery of the New World.

In the thirteenth century, Europe was becoming a geo-political reality. It was true that the term 'Europe' had existed, but in a purely geographical sense—the Western peninsula of Asia— since the seventh century B.C. (we find the term used by a contemporary of Hesiod, and by Herodotus, for example, in the fifth century B.C.). But when, after the battle of Poitiers, the Spaniard Isidore The Young called Charles Martel's army the army of 'Europeans', the geographical definition of Europe began to become an arena of competing political imperatives and new ideological choices, imperatives and choices which reached a remarkable degree of complexity in the thirteenth and fourteenth century.

The emancipation of the serfs and the rebirth of the communal system grouped around traders and artisans in renovated urban centres all contributed to the emergence of a new social partner: the 'people' of the towns, who needed protection from the violence and scornful attitude of the barons, but also from the domination of a whole feudal clergy, and who themselves provoked an anticlerical popular tradition. In France, the king guaranteed the status of many independent communes, and the Paris Parliament played an important role in the centralization of the Capetian state. The convocation of the Estates General by Philippe le Bel in 1302 demonstrated the arrival on the political scene of the Third Estate, established the limits of clerical power; and dealt a fatal blow to the barons.

*　　*　　*

Through the reconstruction of urban centres around the commercial bourgeoisie and the setting up of a communal system based upon administrative autonomy, these new communities became very independent minded and laid the foundations of a new *demos*: communities of citizens under the rule of law, and the guaranteeing of the smooth functioning of trade. In this urban framework, communal schools found themselves in conflict with religious schools (which, however, until the Renaissance, confined themselves to elementary teaching) and began to provide the urban communities with secular scholars, as it were, who could deal with letter writing, the publication of legal documents, public accounting, and so on. As early as the beginning of the thirteenth century these urban communities progressively abandoned Latin in administrative practice in favour of their own national idioms.

Alongside the conflictual unity of royal power and papal authority in the framework of an evolving Europe of nation states, another antagonistic and dynamic symbiosis between political power and ecclesiastical authority began to take place at the very heart of the medieval town. The 'people', the third actor along with the king and the Church, began to undergo internal differentiation, and 'civil society' emerged from its embryonic *polis* and, developing all the time, contributed to the reaffirmation of the notion of equality.

This revival of the urban recreated a political area and, with it, the struggle for its independence. From the twelfth century, politics was rediscovered. Corroborating the thesis that the political and philosophical modes of thought are intimately bound up with one another—both are centred upon Man, Reason, and the City—the urban and communal Middle Ages re-established the importance of both. The child of the universities and their theological debates, political philosophy was reborn and became independent. The 'birth of the secular spirit' the Man-centredness of philosophy took place, therefore, at the heart of theological thought, that is, inside an overall theological interpretation of the world which remained the keystone of all philosophical systems (at least until the successive upheavals and reappraisals of the modern period).

In the same way, the secular community's increasing claim upon power ran parallel to its aspirations and desire to increase its spiritual awareness. In this respect, the Caesaro-Papist will to power expressed by the European kings in the form of the religious fervour of the urban bourgeoisie, inscribed the aspirations of the secular community into the overall religious view of the world. However, the clashes between king and pope, the independence of communal power, and, at another level, Renaissance philosophy itself—the child of the medieval secular spirit—or, at yet another, the Reformation, which led to mysticism and the 'political' spirit of the townspeople, all these factors contributed, each in its own way and always in an ambivalent and sometimes surprising way, to the slow development of the secularization of thought and of European society:

It is the crucial period from the thirteenth to the fourteenth century which saw the creation of the national monarchies of the

West, in England and France above all, and made laboratories of them out of which ultimately emerged that prodigious novelty: representative power. . . . It was an infinitely subtle and in many ways misleading process at the end of which, by means of a continuous reappraisal of traditional categories of mediation and the body politic, and via an extraordinary symbolic alchemy, a complete overturning of the essence of political legitimacy took place.[1]

The secular society issue was, in fact, present at the very beginnings of Christianity which had to posit, in order to survive in the first centuries of its existence, the principle of the separation of faith and the city (which ran parallel with the distinction between the soul and the body). Christ's injunction of 'render unto Ceasar'—which became extremely important in St Paul's writing—added a political dimension to Christianity and to the already dual nature of Christ. Paradoxically, it was by stressing these two orders of things that Christianity gave itself the means of appropriating the political by claiming to offer it its true place within an overall unity. As Georges de Largarde has noted,[2] the 'distinctiveness' of the two domains did not mean their 'independence'. It is in this way that the original duality of the temporal and the spiritual subsequently conditioned the whole of Western political thought; and the organization of the Church around the papacy was also intimately tied to different phases of political organization, and to the dislocation of the Christianized Roman Empire and its eventual replacement by the European nation states.

The process of the secularization of the political is fundamentally paradoxical and pluralistic. The secular view of politics, begun by the intellectual revolution of the nineteenth century, and symbolized by the tryptich Freud–Marx–Nietzsche, advocates atheistic thought, displacing and radically modifying the terms of the political, and effecting a change in the interpretation

[1] Gauchet, M., *Le Désenchantement du monde* (Paris, Gallimard, 1985) p. 200.
[2] Lagarde, G., *La naissance de l'esprit laïque au déclin du Moyen-Age* (Paris, Ed. Béatrice, 1934).

of Man in the world. Even though all traces of the eschatological view were not eradicated in this secular thought, even though teleological thought remained at the heart of certain 'materialist' views of the world and society, the suppression of the ultimate divine basis of things produced a fundamental break, a reversal which meant that, henceforward, it was at the heart of secular thought that the 'disenchantment of the world' took place via the agency of critical thought. From the setting up of the secular state, which was the symbolic expression, made at different times and by different means, of the radical break of the European democracies with their past, the dynamic of Christian thought found itself as if out of play, and the religious view no longer enjoyed the same fundamental dialectical relation to the production of the political.

However, the religious domination of the political carried on under different forms:

> **It is clear that until the end of the nineteenth century, the Church continued to believe that the state was not an end in itself and that its role was to help men reach the celestial city through the practice of and respect for morality. . . . It was not until Leo XIII that the papacy declared that the two powers were totally independent from one another and followed their own objectives. . . . However, the problem of true pontifical doctrine remained complex because the Church did not renounce the objective it had been created for. It intended to continue the same work by different means.**[1]

In fact, after thirty years of the apparent reduction of the influence of the Catholic Church in Europe (from the end of the Second World War when it sanctioned the complicity between the Holy See and Franco and Hitler until the 1970s which saw the stress upon women's liberation and a greater permissiveness), and during which time the Church undertook a major doctrinal review with Vatican II, the papacy became involved, in the 1980s, with John-Paul II's election to the papacy, in a

---

[1] Pacaut, Marcel, *La théocratie, l'Eglise et le pouvoir au Moyen Age* (Paris, Aubier, 1957) p. 220.

wide political redeployment at the international level. The offensive by the Roman Catholic Church coincided with the rise in recent years of various 'fundamentalist' religious movements on the international political scene (Islamic movements, of course, in the Middle East and Africa, fundamentalist Christianity in the United States, fundamentalist Judaism in Israel, and fundamentalist Catholicism in Europe, especially in France).

It is interesting to note that the various fundamentalist movements which interweave the religious with the political share certain characteristics. First, they all develop in periods of economic crisis which increase inequality within a given society and, therefore, create a situation in which violent outbursts can occur. Furthermore, it is beyond dispute that, over the last ten years or so, the emergence or re-emergence of the religious within the political is also linked with a certain retreat on the part of leftist ideologies.

The 'anachronistic' character of the presence of the religious within the political is, of course, more strongly felt in the West than in the Third World. The contrast is also stark between European countries and countries of Islamic cultures. This is because, first of all, the secular tradition, explicitly stressed in France and Italy, for example, or implicitly asserted, as in many Northern European kingdoms, is a 'heavy' component of European culture, whereas in Islam, fundamentalism is rooted in the very tradition of politico-religious power. On the other hand, an important difference between Islamic fundamentalisms and European Catholic fundamentalism should be stressed: the Islamic movements often have an essential popular element within them, and because of their activism which works closely with the mass of the people, they are very distinct from, for example, French 'traditionalist' activism. In this way, fundamentalist activism in Algeria is closer to that of the liberation theology activists of Latin America, than to the troops of, say, 'Christian-solidarity' involved with bringing together and offering relief to the marginalized masses of uneducated uprooted peasants on the edges of the huge cities.

Of course, there is a world of difference between the value-systems of the different movements, especially concerning the notion of equality and, by extension, the status of women. It is worth noting, however, that, in spite of the spectacular and media-dominated demonstrations of the Catholic fundamentalists in Europe, Catholicism is also developing a vast 'social' aspect to its current work concerning 'aid to the Third World', and acts of 'charity' to the European poor, and is developing a network of structures which, through non-governmental organizations, link the official hierarchy with the progressive Catholic 'dissidents' throughout the world. In this way, the Catholic Church maintains its contacts and unites the different strands of the Catholic presence in politics: allied with the extreme right-wing fundamentalists on the question of religious education, the reappraisal of the separation of Church and State, and of moral standards, the Church, nevertheless, uses its links with the 'social' and Third World 'leftist' Catholics in its elaboration of the Christian conception of human rights and republican ideals. In the context of the Western crisis of capitalism, the Catholic Church, with both its 'left-wing' and its 'right-wing' is reorganizing its power and its relation to the political sphere.

The Church, with its high profile, superstar Pope, is attempting to occupy a new strategic position at a time when, in a certain way, Europe finds itself, as it did in the nodal period of the thirteenth and fourteenth centuries, at the crossroads. The restructuring of the world economy in the context of the vast technological and scientific changes, the social changes taking place in the context of profound urban change, the questioning of national and state structures because of the wider European market, the redefining of relations between former colonial powers and the Third World, the clash of cultures within Europe, all these oblige Europe to find a supra-national cohesion. And it is in its global context that, for example, John-Paul II's speech to the European Parliament in 1988 must be situated, a speech in which he stressed Christian religion as the unifying and salvationary element of contemporary Europe. 'If the Christian and religious substratum of this continent were to be marginalized and its ethical and social contribution lost, this would not only be the negation of Europe's past, it would also mean that a future worthy of Europeans—whether believers or not—would be seriously compromised.'[1]

In this way, all the elements of a new 'crusade' for the defence of the Christian West are assembled. The social and political restructuring of Europe in the context of the reactivated competition (mythical or actual) with Islamic culture allows the Church to re-enter the political game with all its diverse currents of thought, theorizations of the political order, and its various attitudes towards the social dimension of things, and which have been reflected in all the various Christian traditions since the Middle Ages. In this way, renewed Thomism confronts renewed political Augustianism; the Dominican and Jesuit schools oppose one another in their struggle for influence both at the philosophical level and on the ground—particularly in Central America.

Of course, the stakes are different from those in the Middle Ages, and the oppositions, realignments, and alliances are new ones. And the clashes take place in different contexts and involve different syntheses. And unlike the situation in the thirteenth and fourteenth centuries—and this is an essential difference— the Christian universalism put forward by the papal vision of the West is today confronted by a competing universalism, that of humanistic atheism; the politico-religious view of Europe which was the only frame of reference for the various medieval versions of the relation between the spiritual and the temporal is now in conflict—potential or actual—with the secular view of the political. If the 'fundamentalism with a human face', of which John-Paul II is the past master, is amusing in some of its most archaic manifestations, it, nevertheless, presents a major challenge to the secular cause, and has installed itself as a real adversary to the secular spirit and its adaptation to the myriad changes taking place in the present period. Whether it is in Eastern Europe, where the challenge to the Soviet 'model' is now demonstrably clear, in the Third World, where Third World

---

[1] See *Le Monde*, 12 October 1988.

Marxism, or orthodox Marxism-Leninism, have not provided a
solution to those crushed by the capitalist system, or else in
Europe where the Welfare State seems to have reached its limits
with the realignments taking place within capitalism, the Christian re-evaluation of an overall vision of the world is now in a
position to fill the theoretical vacuum and accompany, support,
comfort and reinforce the painful reorientation of world capitalism.

With the resurgence of the principle of the *major et sanior
pars* and the multiplication of various 'commissions of wise men',
'technocracies', 'politocracies', and 'ad-hocracies', the Church
too claims more and more openly its place as 'religious authority'
in the gallery of 'moral authorities'. Moreover, while diminishing
the traditional idea of tolerance and heightening that of the 'true
character' of 'cultural identities', the Church is apparently trying
to challenge even the principle of separation of Church from
State, a separation that is in no sense uniform given the various
national histories in Europe and the diversity of legislation pertaining to this issue.

Faced with these various challenges, the secular, whose original meaning was to make politics 'everybody's business', must
both re-evaluate and recharge itself, as it were, by reappraising
its own history. It has to renovate itself, and put forward a new
critical view and perspective of democracy in the present period.
Secularism is essentially a dividing instrument: it distinguishes
what is related to public affairs from what is related to the private; it defines the relations between the collective and the
individual, it defends rationality while yet protecting that other
different order—the irrational, the inexplicable. It is the principle of the secular upon which the definition of democratic
progress is now based, no longer conceived in terms of the ultimate transcendence of all contradictions, but rather as an undertaking that is perpetually renewed in response to economic,
social and cultural changes. It takes into account the antagon-
isms at work in a society, strives for the reduction of inequality,
and for the promotion of new modes of participation for everyone in political decision-making.

This opening brought about by secularization has its origins, of course, in that period which saw 'the movement from a closed world to an infinite universe',[1] that is to say, the Middle Ages which ended on the threshold of the New World, and under the sky of Galileo Galilei and Giordano Bruno. The Middle Ages allowed us to open this fabulous book that Jorge de Burgos had hidden in the library-labyrinth of the *Name of the Rose*, a book which 'could teach learned men the clever and, from that moment illustrious artifices that could legitimatise the reversal' of relations of domination, the book that 'could teach that freeing onself of the fear of the Devil is wisdom'.[2]

[1] Koyré, A. *Du monde clos à l'univers infini* (Paris, Gallimard, 1973).
[2] Eco, Umberto, *op. cit.* p. 474.

Islamic Associations and Europe

Bruno Etienne*

Religious practice in Europe

The Muslim community is perceived above all as a source of immigrant labour. It is difficult for this reason to respond to the apparently simple question: how many Muslims are there in Europe? Commitment to the Islamic faith is not a factor which is taken account of in the official statistics of European states or of Islamic associations in Europe. The sole exception to this is Switzerland, where the ten-yearly census includes a register of the religions to which residents hold. The figure of six and a half million Muslims that is normally cited for Western Europe is arrived at simply by adding the numbers of immigrants from Muslim countries. This method, though it is inaccurate in the results which it yields, gives some idea of the scale of the question. In the following tables, I have thought it useful to include the figures for Muslims in Eastern Europe, since a long-term trend towards rapprochement with the West is already evident in the thriving commercial co-operation between the two spheres. The statistics are drawn from different sources; this explains a number of disparities, for example between France and Germany, in relation to other available statistics. What I have done, in fact, is to take the average in cases where there is extreme variation—as in the case of France, for instance, where

* Bruno Etienne is Professor at the Institute for Political Studies in Aix-en-Provence. He is co-organizer of DEA Arab World, and is the author of several books on Islam, most notably *L'Islamisme radical* (Paris, Hachette, 1987) and *La France et l'Islam* (Paris, Hachette, 1989).

Muslims in Europe

Northern Europe

Sweden	22 000
Denmark	18 000
Norway	6 000
Finland	1 350
Iceland	500

Eastern Europe

Yugoslavia	3 000 000
Albania	1 700 000
Bulgaria	800 000
Greece	150 000
Czechoslovakia	150 000
Cyprus	117 000
Austria	86 000
Romania	50 000
Germany	15 000
Poland	2 000
Hungary	100

Western Europe

France	2 450 000
Germany	1 700 000
Great Britain	800 000
Netherlands	300 000
Belgium	250 000
Italy	200 000
Switzerland	55 000
Spain	15 000
Portugal	15 000
Gibraltar	3 000
Luxemburg	1 000
Ireland	500
Malta	100

Breakdown According to Country of Origin

FRANCE

The magazine *Hommes et migrations* has published a new set of statistics for foreigners in France: 'Vérités statistiques sur l'immigration' (1984). Traditionally Islamic countries of origin can be broken down thus:

Algeria	822 037
Cameroon	18 807
Congo	13 223
Ivory Coast	15 241
Mali	33 431
Morocco	555 871
Senegal	42 102
Tunisia	235 257
Turkey	150 031
Yugoslavia	78 316

The 1982 census shows:

Iran	10 420
Lebanon	11,200

P. Balta, in his book *L'islam dans le monde*:

French converts	40 000

It has been estimated that one Muslim in five in France is an Arab. Apart from converts there are about a million French Muslims:

ex-harkis (Algerian)	450 000
children of immigrants	600 000

NETHERLANDS

In 1979 the breakdown was as follows:

Morocco	62 100
Tunisia	1 900
Turkey	103 800
Surinam	?
Yugoslavia	?

BELGIUM

In 1981, Muslims (205 000 + 4 000 illegal residents) accounted for around 21% of the foreign population.

Countries of origin:

Algeria	12 000
Morocco	108 000
Tunisia	9 000
Turkey	67 000
Yugoslavia	4 000
Others	5 000

WEST GERMANY

In 1979 Muslims (1 700 000) accounted for 30% of foreign residents.

Countries of origin:

Algeria	4 900
Morocco	31 900
Tunisia	20 700
Turkey	1 268 300
Yugoslavia	?

SPAIN

Spanish converts	3 000
Algeria, Tunisia, Libya	16 000
Black Africa	12 000
Iraq	3 500
Iran	7,500
Jordan	5 500
Syria	6 000
Palestine	2 000
Morocco	126 000
Pakistan	4 000
Afghanistan	1 000
Egypt	1 500
Lebanon	4 000
Total	192 000

GREAT BRITAIN

The Muslim population is estimated at 852 000, almost all of whom have British nationality.

Countries of origin:

Bangladesh	64 000
Egypt	34 000
India	84 000
Iran	50 000
Kenya	52 000
Libya	11 000
Malawi	12 000
Morocco	10 000
Nigeria	25 000
Pakistan	357 000
Near East	66 000
Tanzania	20 000
Turkey	21 000
Uganda	15 000
Others	27 000

IMMIGRANTS IN CONTINENTAL EUROPE
(in thousands)

	Netherlands	Sweden	France	FRG	Belgium	Switzerland
	1986	*1986*	*1982*	*1986*	*1984*	*1985*
Austrian	3	2.8	2.7	174.2		28.8
Finnish	0.6	134.2	1	10.1		1.4
Spanish	18.2	2.8	321.4	151	55.1	110.4
Greek	3.8	8	7.9	278.5	20.7	8.5
Italian	17	3.9	333.7	535.5	269.3	388.4
Portuguese	7.5	1.5	764.9	77	10.4	39.2
Turkish	160.6	21.9	123.5	1 425.7	72.5	52.8
Yugoslavian	11.6	38.4	64.4	591.1	5.3	77.4
Algerian	0.6	0.5	795.8	5.4	10.8	1.9
Moroccan	122.7	1	431.1	51	123.2	1.6
Tunisian	2.6	0.7	189.4	23.6	6.8	2.2
Others	219.8	175.1	655.8	1 158.8	323.5	243.4
Total	**568**	**390.8**	**3 680.1**	**4 482.6**	**897.6**	**956**
Percentage of total population	**3.90%**	**4.60%**	**6.80%**	**7.40%**	**9.10%**	**14.70%**

the figure cited for Muslim residents varies from two to six million. . . .

From the foregoing statistics, a number of points arise:

• The greatest difficulty, in the case of France certainly,[1] lies in defining what is meant by 'Muslim'.[2]
• There are more 'Muslims' in the other EEC countries taken together than in France.
• The countries of Eastern Europe are experiencing a similar phenomenon, since the Muslim population totals upwards of six million there too, if one counts Albania. It may be pointed out that the Yugoslav leader, Raif Dizdarevic, is a Muslim from Bosnia.

[1] See my *La France et i'islam* (Paris, Hachette, 1989).
[2] The means whereby immigrants are labelled 'Muslim' do not correspond to the anthropological method of inquiry which distinguishes the devout, pious, practising Muslim from the non-practising, the atheist from the proselyte, etc.

• The tables do not take account of Muslims who are French, British, or Belgian nationals.
• Turkey features not as an EEC partner but as a source of manpower for West Germany. Switzerland, whilst not being a Community member state, is nonetheless counted in with Western Europe.

There is some need, then, to refine these data by setting them against more precisely measured categories of foreigners and *émigrés*, specifying clearly the countries of origin in question, since there are numerous immigrants from EEC countries too.

If we add up the 'potential Muslims' (Algerians, Moroccans, Tunisians, and Turks), we obtain a figure of around a million and a half, the same figure as we find for immigrants from the southern countries of Europe such as Spain, Portugal, Italy, Greece, and Yugoslavia (some of whom may themselves, indeed, be Muslims . . .). Might a more precise figure be obtained by taking account of differences in religious status?

This transplanted Islam, which escapes statistical measurement but is a visible social reality, is becoming more and more established. Those Muslims who decide to remain for political or economic reasons organize themselves into cultural and religious communities according to their national, linguistic, or traditional Islamic origins. Thus the 'Office for Religious Affairs' (*Diyanet iseleri Baskanligi*) opened a 'Western Europe' section in Ankara in 1984, and a large Central Office in Cologne on 13 May 1985. The latter was set up to minister to the religious needs of Turkish Muslims throughout Western Europe. This Office appoints and oversees the imams, and assumes full responsibility for coordinating activities on a regional and international basis. It comes as something of a surprise to note that the only lay Muslim state should thus take charge of religious affairs, whilst countries like Algeria and Morocco find it difficult to exercise any similar control over their citizens living in France. The Turkish approach extends in precisely the form described to France, where Turkish Muslims come under the jurisdiction of officials who are nominated and overseen by the Turkish Embassy.

The case of Turkey is quite unique. It is more useful to consider in this context a number of major Islamic associations. The Muslim World Congress, set up in 1926 after the abolition of the Caliphate by Attaturk, set out to unite Muslims throughout the world. Based at present in Pakistan, but extending throughout Europe too, this body fulfils what is essentially a missionary role, offering organized support to all Muslim minorities. The World Muslim League, founded at Mecca in 1962, has as its function the coordinating and financing of Islamic centres throughout the world. Some years ago, it opened a central office in Paris. This office works in association with the Great Mosque in Brussels, where meetings for imams from all over Europe have been held since 1983. In similar vein, the Conference of Foreign Ministers undertook in the early 1970s to found an Islamic Council of Europe. Based in London, this body had been active since 1973. It aims to provide a positive image of Islam in Europe, and to provide a coordinating and advisory service for the different Islamic organizations in the West. In my *Islamisme radical*, I described the suspicion with which I view this organization, for it seems to me to be run on quite undemocratic, not to say 'fundamentalist', grounds and to constitute an obstacle to the integration of Muslims whom it wishes to control in the interests of a number of states.

The chief argument over the setting up of a Muslim Federation in France can be drawn from what I have just outlined as the activities of these different organizations. It seems to me quite out of the question and altogether undesirable that a sovereign state should submit to such interference in its religious affairs. Muslim countries, moreover, do not admit such interference in their own affairs. If Saudi Arabia were to adopt a pluralistic approach to religion—which is a wholly unrealistic hypothesis— then there might be a case for revising our attitude. As things stand, however, the countries of Europe are giving way to black- mail over the supply of oil and accepting the present state of affairs because Saudi Arabia is the West's only ally among the Arab states of the Middle East and in OPEC. Civic morality, I am afraid, is not taken into consideration. . . . The Arab League seeks other means of mobilizing support for the Arab cause (see below, for example, the document produced by the League's Ambassador to Paris). Nor is it France alone who should be concerned by the seriousness of all of this: it is a global issue, in keeping with the universalistic and messianic objectives of Islam. The knock-on effect should be clear for all to see.

While taking up residence in host countries, Muslims retain their bonds with the Muslim community throughout the world. There are clear signs of a move towards permanent settlement in the countries in question. Local Muslim associations are no longer content to rent premises for prayer meetings; now they buy. The money comes from gifts, alms (*zakât*), state hand-outs—in particular from Saudi Arabia—and Islamic organi-zations throughout the world. Considerable sums of money are passed around in this way. The buildings concerned are trans-formed into veritable centres of Islamic culture: places in which to meet and pray, where adults are offered educational oppor-tunities and children Koranic instruction. And all the while great Cathedral-like mosques are springing up in Rome, in Madrid, and elsewhere.

Muslims have also made inroads into the printing world. They now produce dailies, weeklies, and books in European lan-guages. Such publications are far from providing the same view of Islam or of the world-wide Muslim community. The magazine *L'islam et l'Occident* (Vienna) presents the image of a 'reformed' Islam which seeks to address the vital question posed by Muslims in a non-Islamic world. On the other hand, such magazines as *Al-Islam* (Munich) or *Quiblah* (La Haye) have an altogether different objective. The view they defend is that of a fundamen-talist Islam which must undergo no modification, regardless of the environmental pressures brought to bear upon immigrants. Presenting themselves as the mouthpieces of tradition (*sunna*), such publications call for a system of Islamic education in order to help younger generations to remain within Muslim tradition and to reject the liberal and individualistic values propounded by the so-called Christian West. A school of just this type is due to open shortly in Paris.

Given the widespread presence of 'potential' Muslims, and in view of the fact that 1992 will bring about some need for harmonization in this domain, it is essential to consider briefly at this point the relative status of the various religions in the different countries of the Community.

The relative status of religions

The most serious obstacle in seeking to asses the relative status of religions is the degree to which the Muslim community lacks any uniform profile. Among the variety of systems which operate within the different countries of the EEC, that of Belgium is the most advanced and the richest in lessons for France.[1] Belgium grants Muslims the same legal rights as Catholics, Jews, and Protestants. A law passed on 14 July 1974 sets out terms for cooperation between the Belgian state and official Islamic organizations. In cases where the Muslim communities do not have the necessary resources, the state pays the imams, and grants financial aid for the construction and upkeep of the buildings and for the accommodation of religious officials. Since 1975, the Education Ministry has prescribed religious courses where these have been requested by parents: at present, over 45% of Muslim children receive this type of instruction, 280 teachers being brought in to cover 700 insitutions that fall within the Ministry's control.

Though half of the schools in Belgium are 'Catholic', there are more Muslim than Christian children in certain local districts. The authorities in a number of dioceses have expressed their readiness to engage a muslim teacher for the courses in Islamic instruction. In several schools in Brussels where the experiment has been tried, however, it has failed due to the influence of the imams and the content of courses which could not be deemed conducive to good relations with the wider community.

[1] Cf. the studies of Albert Bastenier and Felice Dassetto: *L'islam transplanté* (Brussels: EPO, 1984) and *Europa nuova frontiera dell'islam* (Rome: Ed. Lavore, 1988).

While Christians and Jews are represented at the communal level, Muslims have recourse to provincial authorities. They do not have an organization which extends over a large geographical base, covering several regions for example. The state stipulates, moreover, that some central body must act as overall representative, a condition which Muslim communities find difficulty in meeting. To resolve the situation, after much toing and froing and three years of parliamentary debate, Belgian common law was extended to cover Islamic institutions. Diplomatic considerations played a role in the matter, since it was thought that the status of Brussels would be enhanced as an international centre and that the Islamic World League might act as a negotiating body. Belgium thus recognizes the imam of the Brussels mosque as the chief imam; this has been met with approval in the embassies of traditional Islamic states. Turkey alone has insisted upon its own independent system. As a logical consequence, the 'Islamic Culture and Religion' association which acted as a forum for opponents of the chief imam was dissolved by the state in 1986. Since then, the imam of Brussels alone has been entrusted with responsibility for Islamic affairs. He it is who nominates the imams and the religious teachers in officially designated schools. Those bodies, however, which have responsibility for secular matters in the Muslim communities are constituted according to legislation and a number of royal ordinances which have come into effect since 1978. Such bodies are democratically elected. Belgium, therefore, offers an example of the 'consistorial' system which I would like to see operate in France. The law of 1981 also makes provision for the salaries of Muslim clergy on a similar basis to bishops, priests, etc. Though it might be argued that there is no clergy in Islam, my feeling is that the prospect of a salary and of a full legal and symbolic staus as legitimate religious agents will bring about the creation of a clerical body that will quickly become 'Weberian', that is to say that there will be no conflict between the idea of clerics managing the funds and that of clerics preaching the scriptures.

In the Netherlands, Church and State are separate. The legal status of the Church was set out in 1853. In theory, Muslims here can benefit from this legal status as a religious community. Until now, however, they have proved resistant to this idea. In order to qualify for state aid, Muslims have chosen instead to present their case as a Social and Cultural Association.

Great Britain has granted passports to a great many Muslims. By becoming British citizens, Muslims enjoy the full range of civil and political rights, including freedom of worship. This does not mean, however, that problems do not arise, in particular over typically Islamic practices such as the slaughter of animals and Islamic religious instruction. The courts have, moreover, categorically rejected requests by British Muslims to implement full Islamic law within the family.

The situation in Germany and Austria is more complex. In these countries, the legal status of religious communities does not depend upon central government but upon each of the federated states. This should provide greater possibilities for Muslims. Until now, Islamic communities have had the status of an approved and registered 'association'. Discussions are underway with a view to obtaining recognition as a 'Publicly Validated Corporation' (KOR). The conditions that must be fulfilled in order to qualify for such status are not inconsiderable:

• the group must have a representative role in the country and a structured hierarchy;
• a guarantee of duration must be provided;
• if several organizations submit requests, the doctrinal differences between them must be clearly defined.

The first application for KOR status was made by the Islamic Community of Germany in 1977. The Minister of Culture for Baden Würtemberg refused it on the grounds that this body did not represent the Muslim community as a whole, and that it was not certain that other groups would join with it. Another such application was put forward to the Minister of Culture in Düsseldorf in 1979 by the Islamic Cultural Centre of Cologne. In Austria, the Islamic community of 'Vienna, Lower-Austria-Burgenland' has had KOR status since 1979. This was a necessary condition in order to have Islamic education in public schools.

Switzerland is, as we know, a confederation made up of twenty-six cantons which all enjoy a very considerable independence. Throughout the course of Switzerland's history, each canton has evolved its own 'ecclesiastical' laws and set up its own legal rights in relation to religious practice. Thus it is, for example, that the cantons of Geneva and Neufchâtel have instituted the separation of Church and State. All ecclesiastical bodies are organized on the basis of private rights. In the Vaud canton, on the other hand, the Evangelical Reformist Church is recognized as a 'national institution' subject to public law.

In a referendum held on 2 March 1980, 79% of the Swiss who voted stated their desire to see closer cooperation betwen the Churches and the State. In the majority of cantons, however, the Churches have the legal status of a public corporation. Until now, Muslims have not sought this status. They have organized themselves into associations locally—very rarely at cantonal level—on the basis of language and nationality. Islamic associations in Switzerland suffer from a lack of active, militant members. Put another way, this means that Muslims in certain European countries are not much more actively devoted to their religion than are those in France. By contrast, it seems clear that the younger generations born to Muslim immigrant parents have a behaviour pattern (in particular with regard to their musical tastes) that can be seen across all of the countries of Europe and which is part of the new identity which such generations are in the process of constructing.

The case of France

The French common law system is founded upon two major principles: freedom of association and the non-intervention of the State. The State does not intervene in Church matters and allows religious communities to organize themselves according to their own statutes and the basic exigencies of the law. There are legal requirements which must be met in relation to Church assets, the management of funds, legal representation and so on. The clauses of common law which bear upon the foregoing were set out in the 1905 legislation on cultural associations, the broad lines of which are the same as those prescribed in an earlier law of 31 July 1901 on freedom of association. The 1905 legislation aimed to provide a framework of legal support for the temporal affairs of religious communities. The separation of Church and State is the overriding feature in the legislation of 1901 and 1905 alike. In accordance with this legislation, the State does not interfere in matters of Church hierarchy, nor in the activities of religions and their ministers. The only constraints placed upon the latter relate to public order such as it is defined by the State.

It is clear from this that the role of the Republic is reduced to a strict minimum, and that Muslims should be expected to comply with this. What would be the outcome if the Muslim community were to adopt a posture similar to that of the Catholic Church? If the latter has benefited from the pros and cons of the situation as defined above, why should Muslims stand to gain nothing?

What appears to be a disadvantage in the case of the Catholic Church seems indeed to be a positive advantage for Muslims. The ecclesiastical hierarcy of the Catholic Church is very particular, and does not easily lend itself to comparison with the structures of the State or with those organizational structures provided for by the two items of legislation discussed above. It is only by distorting its nature as an organization that the Catholic Church can be made to fit the mould in question. The parish priest is not automatically elected by the administrative council of the diocesan association, nor indeed is the bishop. It would appear, instead, that the terms of the legislation laid down are more suited to the 'protestant' and Jewish communions, with their more 'federative' structures and the role therein of consistory and rabbinate. It is difficult not to conclude that the framework described would lend itself well to a Muslim 'church' organized into 'lay' federations. This would obviate the need for the creation of a clergy as such, since those officials charged with responsibility for the various federative 'branches' of the religion could be laymen elected alongside the imams, the latter being organized on the lines of the Jewish rabbinate. Neither imams, nor rabbis, nor pastors would discharge their function as 'priests' in the Catholic sense of the term.

The other major problem which arises from taking the Catholic religion as a model lies in the designation of Church hierarchy. The pontiff clears with the French government that there are no political objections to the designation of bishops and, more particularly, of cardinals. This practice is in line with canon law, but has no basis in legislation laid down by the French state. I cannot conceive of the University of Al-Azhar seeking such ratification for the nomination of the imam of Aix-en-Provence of Saudi Arabia's Minister of Religion clearing the matter with the French ambassador. As we know, the Leagues finance clerics and mosques at their own discretion—a practice which as G. Kepel[1] has shown, does not always bring about the desired results. Thus the Islamic World League failed in its bid to set up a national Islamic Centre in Lyon which would have ousted Paris and Algeria as the major centres of Muslim influence in France. It matters little whether such attempts succeed or fail: what is at stake here is an unacceptable level of interference in the internal affairs of France which must be halted by the French government. Whilst one cannot withhold from foreign states the right to provide funding for places of worship and charitable activities, this must be granted only on condition that the states in question go through the French government and conduct their affairs in accordance with the laws relating to associations, whether French of foreign. I do not see Saudi Arabia, for its part, putting up with any Christian organization providing funds to set up monasteries in the desert of the 'happy' peninsula.

We must, therefore, recognize the advantages offered by the 1905 legislation. The liberal conditions set out in relation to the separate identity and the status of religious institutions are surprising, not to say unique, in their scope. There is no bar to the free movement of religious officials, and no limits to their freedom of association; nor does any *exequatur* or *imprimatur* inhibit the publication and implementation of the rulings of

---

[1] *Les banlieues de l'islam* (Paris: Ed. du Seuil, 1988).

religious authorities. In other words, the lay Republic is much more tolerant than the Church itself, and the Pope may come to France to lobby against contraception even though the law of the land permits it. Muslims must, like their Protestant and Jewish counterparts, learn to benefit from wide-ranging liberties that are as open to Islam as to any other institutionalized creed. If religious organizations respect the rule of law, then there is no bar to their activities in matters religious, charitable, cultural, or educational, no bar, in a word, to their freedom to proselytize. In this sense, the French episcopacy has very ably exploited the Ferry Law on the teaching of the catechism in schools, and Muslims should seek to do likewise.

Those who oppose the statutory definition of the Church accuse it of diluting the specificity of religious worship and making it merely subject to the laws that govern social, cultural, and charitable activities in general. I think, in fact, that the opposite can be proved, and that this helps us to understand why Islam can be seen as having failed to distinguish between the spheres of public and private interests. The spiritual realm in France is clearly separated from the Church temporal, for any activities which do not fall within the purview of the 1905 legislation must be deemed not to be 'religious' in any strict sense of the term. To that extent, such activities remain subject to the same liberties and the same constraints as any other private concern. This distinction within the Church itself between the clerical and the secular allows religious institutions to receive public funding, whilst the same funding would be legally prohibited on purely religious grounds due to the lay character of the State. It is only a dishonest or ill-informed rational which could argue the opposite; it is clear that all of those responsible for managing Church funds well understand the possibilities offered by this dual mechanism. The finer points of any legislation in this matter depend upon how well we define the notion of culture. We should understand this term, however, in its broadest sense as comprising a religious worship which alone escapes the jurisdiction of the State. The courts themselves refuse to pass judgment on any specifically religious litigation that comes before them, even when this relates to the premises occupied by a religious organization. It is ironic to note that Catholic fundamentalists are quite willing to have recourse to the processes of justice within the reviled Republic.

The power of mayors is strictly limited, therefore, to policing and maintaining order in matters relating to the public demonstration of religious faith. Many invoke this power wrongly by refusing to allow places of Muslim worship to be set up, the argument being (as I had occasion to witness in a case in Marsille) that those associations seeking to establish premises are not covered either by the 1901 or the 1905 legislation. Even fire officers have been known to get involved in such matters if the fire escapes are not adjudged to meet the standard requirements. These are examples of so many obstacles which could easily be removed by legal means. What is more, the refusal to accede to the requests of Muslim communities may have serious electoral consequences, given that there is now a 'French-Muslim' vote which can shift the balance of power in certain districts—though my feeling is that such a vote will very quickly lose its clearly defined profile and become dissipated like its counterparts, the 'Jewish' or ex-settler vote. I believe that immigrant communities, once integrated, will vote according to class interests: there is no such thing as a second generation immigrant ('Beur') vote! In the meantime, the questions of cultural and legal status can be exploited to advantage; this has been done already by the Catholic and, increasingly, the Jewish communities. Numerous items of legislation have modified the laws discussed above: one can cite the decrees of 16 March 1906 and 17 March 1970, or the laws of 2 January 1907 and 29 July 1961, which relate, among other things, to the management of religious associations and confessional education, or the law of 24 July 1987 on patronage, which allows for taxes to be levied against religious donations—though indirect aid to religious institutions is a commonly established practice.

More significantly, the 'European convention for the Protection of Human Rights and Fundamental Liberties' (ratified by the law of 31 December 1973 and made public by the decree of

3 May 1974) has superseded almost every aspect of the 1905 legislation by recognizing each individual's right to manifest their faith or religion, individually or collectively, in public or in private, through worship, education, practice or ritual. But every right presupposes the funding required to assure its enjoyment.

Over one particular aspect—education—doubt continues to hang. The definition of what is religious is not necessarily the same for State and Church alike. The catechism, certainly, does not come under the rules governing education to the extent that the latter remains, in its most profane sense, free, secular and obligatory. Nor is there any consensus on this whole question. Yet it must be said that the State—even at its most authoritarian—seems far more liberal on this issue than the Catholic Church, which uses and abuses its freedom in this domain, even to the point, it is to be feared, of instituting a tax payable by all to ensure that Catholic instruction becomes once again a commodity that is to be paid for rather than being provided free. The subtlety with which the Catholic Church exploits its pre-eminence is evident throughout Europe as a whole. No Church, of course, will ever be totally independent of the State; but we should recognize that in France, as in Orwell's *Animal Farm*, there is one Church that is more equal than the others. There is nothing unrealistic about the desire to see the separation of Church and State redefined along lines that are equally favourable to all. In this way, all Churches would enjoy equivalent status, and their relations with one another and with the State would constitute a real dialogue and would enhance the prospects for a harmonious society.

The Papal Spiderweb

*Penny Lernoux**

More than a decade into the reign of Pope John Paul II, it is obvious to even the most reluctant papal critics that he is determined to undo the reforms that have made Catholicism a more relevant religion in the First World and an instrument for popular empowerment in the Third. The effects of John Paul's 'restoration' have already been felt in Latin America and the United States, where he has achieved what the White House could not by slowing down or destroying the careers of activist Catholic leaders who challenged US military and business interests. At the time of his election in 1978, however, few could have foreseen the extent to which a Polish authoritarian would reshape the world's largest church or galvanize the international Catholic right wing. As the Pope himself commented shortly after his election, the 'eminent cardinals' who had chosen him did not know 'what sort of man I am'.

The cardinals, like many others, mistakenly believed that because John Paul had participated in the Second Vatican Council (Vatican II) in the early 1960s, he would continue its reforms. But they underestimated the Polish factor: in Poland's hierarchical church, Catholics are expected to obey a clerical caste; no dissent is allowed. Although such discipline has enabled the church to survive and even flourish in a Communist state, it has also produced a narrow, fundamentalist religion. 'For the Pope and those who think as he does', said one Vatican analyst,

* Penny Lernoux is *The Nation's* Latin America correspondent. This article is adapted from her new book, *People of God* (Viking, New York, 1989).

'Eastern Europe is where the old-time religion has been pre-
served—ironically, thanks to Communism'. John Paul's rigid
anti-Communism 'likewise reflects his Polish background'. Dis-
trustful of the pluralism in democracies, he is also suspicious of
those who oppose strongly anti-Communist dictatorships, such
as the progressive bishops and priests of Chile.

John Paul's world view, which some US bishops liken to that
of former President Ronald Reagan, might have been better
understood had more people been aware of his association with
Opus Dei, a secretive Catholic movement that gained ascendancy in Franco's Spain. As Archbishop of Kraków, John Paul
visited Opus Dei centres in Europe, and a collection of his
speeches at these gatherings was published by Opus and sent to
the Vatican Secretariat of State. At the time of the funeral of
John Paul I, the future Pontiff made a pilgrimage to the Roman
Tomb of Msgr. José María Escrivá de Balaguer, Opus Dei's
founder.

'The Work', as Opus Dei is popularly known, is heartily dis-
liked by many bishops for its secretiveness, intrigue and right-
wing tendencies, and earlier Popes kept it at arm's length. But
upon his accession, John Paul II elevated Opus to a worldwide
prelature, giving it the status of a major religious order, such as
the Jesuits. It has since formed part of a powerful group of
Catholic organizations, some of US origin, that promote the
Pope's political agenda—and that of US conservatives.

'Opus responds . . . to the Pope's idea of creating an army of
lay people who are both consecrated and at the same time capable of being active in the temporal world under Rome's control', explained Juan Arias, Vatican correspondent for the
Spanish newspaper *El País*. 'He likes their activism, their anti-
Communism, their internal compactness where no plurality of
ideas exists.' Opus also responds to John Paul's yearnings for
the 'perfect society'—to quote a phrase he often uses—of the
Middle Ages, when church and state were inseparable and the
church was the only source of spiritual salvation. This is known
as integralism, and although most Americans have probably
never heard the word, it is familiar in Europe and Latin America,

which have experienced fascist corporate states. Such governments trace their roots to the medieval estates and guilds: instead
of political parties, different sectors of society (for example,
capital, labour, farmers, and professionals) are supposed to be
represented by modern versions of the guilds, although in practice, under Franco, Mussolini and, more recently, Gen. Augusto
Pinochet, only the capitalists and the landowning classes have
benefited. Such a system has held considerable appeal for the
Catholic Church, which has lost much of its earlier power
through the rise of labour movements and political parties that
espouse socialism and democratic egalitarianism. The forerun-
ners of fascism in Spain, France, Germany, and Austria, playing
on middle- and upper-class fears of political domination by the
masses, portrayed themselves as the champions of law and order,
Christian morality, and private property. These fears were
shared by Catholic leaders who, when the old order of the aristocracy gave way, tended to align themselves with the new inte-
gralists.

John Paul appears to believe that the Vatican can impose its
perfect society on a late-twentieth-century world, absurd though
this may seem. In 1987, for example, he forced the Italian bishops to take a partisan stand on behalf of the Christian Democrats
during the general election campaign. After Vatican II the bishops, led by Pope Paul VI, had distanced themselves from Italian
politics, but John Paul insisted on dragging them back into the
fray, thereby ending a twenty-five-year tradition of nonpartisan-
ship. Papal loyalists in the United States, such as New York's
John Cardinal O'Connor and Boston's Bernard Cardinal Law,
have followed a similar line, insisting that Catholic politicians
uphold Rome's teachings against abortion and divorce or face
ostracism from the local church. But the Pope's political
ambitions may not be limited to social issues: according to one
well-informed US archbishop, Rome hopes for the eventual
establishment of a Catholic Party of the United States similar to
the Christian Democratic parties of Europe and Latin America.

Opus Dei, with its integralist outlook, is a good example of
the Pope's political and religious ambitions. Although it has not

attracted many recruits in the United States—about 3000—it enjoys the support of similarly elitist Catholic organizations that draw their membership heavily from the Republican corporate right, such as the Knights of Malta. Opus is more active and influential in Europe and Latin America, particularly in Spain, Italy, Chile, Peru, Columbia, and Mexico. According to Opus spokesmen, the movement's 74,000 members direct or influence 487 universities and high schools in eighty-seven countries, as well as fifty-two radio and television stations, 694 publications, thirty-eight news and publicity agencies, and twelve film and distribution companies. (Opus-controlled universities place strong emphasis on journalism.) Most members are well-to-do professionals—Opus purposefully recruits among the rising middle classes—and some have held high positions in their countries' governments. In Chile, for instance, Opus members and sympathizers were among those who supported the Central Intelligence Agency-backed coup that overthrew President Salvador Allende. Hernán Cubillos, who founded *Qué Pasa*, a magazine under Opus Dei's influence, became General Pinochet's Minister of Foreign Relations. He was later identified in a number of news reports as having close links with the CIA.

Opus 'serves a function for the political right and power holders', said a student of the movement in Latin America. 'Its strong endorsement of a class society can also be used as a rationale by the middle and upper classes to justify their life styles, even though they may not be members. And because it serves the purpose of the upper classes, it is able to exert an influence on the political and economic situation.' A Spanish priest made a similar observation about the influence of Opus bankers and industrialists in Europe: 'They want to stop the growth of socialism and pacify the labour movement through religion'.

Although Opus Dei's beginnings were relatively humble, the charismatic personality of its founder, Monsignor Escrivá, opened doors to the influential and wealthy. Born in 1902 in a small town at the foot of the Spanish Pyrenees, Escrivá was the son of a tradesman. In those days the priesthood was one of the few openings to higher education for Spain's poorer classes, and

when Escrivá entered a seminary he also began work toward a
law degree. By 1925 he was both lawyer and priest. In 1928,
while celebrating mass, he had a celestial vision telling him to
form Opus Dei. The vision was coloured by Spanish asceticism
and Escrivá's longing to cleanse the world of sinfulness. Physical
mortification—one of the more controversial Opus practices—
was not uncommon at the time among traditional Spanish Catholics, but Escrivá tended to overdo it. He frequently flagellated
himself so violently that his bathroom walls were spattered with
blood. For most of his life he wore a 'cilice', a metal chain with
sharp tips that prick the skin, Opus Dei's preferred instrument
of self-torment.

Escrivá was also influenced by the Spanish Civil War, which
interrupted his plans for the movement and unleashed massive
persecution of the church. He fled to Burgos, which was controlled by Franco's forces, and there wrote his most famous
work, *The Way*, a compendium of 999 maxims that became
Opus Dei's spiritual handbook. The civil war intensified his
militant anti-Communism, but he was also impelled towards the
political right by the longing of a *petit bourgeois* to be accepted
by the aristocracy. In 1968 he successfully petitioned the government for a title that had belonged to an eighteenth-century
nobleman. The same elitism was reflected in Opus Dei's rigid
hierarchy and its early emphasis on recruiting from the 'intellectual' class—those with university degrees. Escrivá saw himself
as a latter-day knight, leading the faithful into battle against
godless Communism. It was for this war that he needed educated
men who would influence and change society, intellectuals who
would assume command of government, industry and finance.
Escrivá used money and the aristocratic title to persuade people
to adopt his conservative brand of Catholicism. Those not convinced, who did not understand the need to be saved, would
learn through 'holy coercion' and 'holy forcefulness.'

Asceticism, anti-Communism, rigid hierarchicalism and
religious militancy thus became the distinguishing marks of
Opus Dei. But secrecy—another characteristic of the Work—
has earned it considerable disrepute. Internal documents and the

testimony of former members show that, unlike most religious orders. Opus has followed a deliberate policy of keeping its membership, hierarchy, rituals, and rules hidden. Many former members say that if they had known what they were getting into they would not have joined. Until 1982 the minimum recruiting age was 15; it has since been raised to 17, but one former official said that Opus recruiters continue to lure children of 8 or 10 into its clubs. The recruitment of minors raised strong feelings in some church circles. In response to parents' concern that the Work had alienated their children, a 1981 directive by England's Basil Cardinal Hume advised the movement not to recruit people under the age of 18.

Escrivá's mania for secrecy reflected his conviction that in a society like Spain's with its strong strains of anti-clericalism, recruiting would be easier if performed by lay people who did not identify themselves with a priestly caste or religious organization. But what began as a tactic developed into an elaborate facade for dictatorial powers, as shown by the secrecy surrounding the 479-article Constitutions that governed the membership completely between 1950 and 1982, and apparently continue to do so in part. (In 1982 a Codex, a new constitution, was promulgated, but in a concluding article it states that the Constitutions will continue in effect for all the obligations not covered in the Codex. Those obligations, described in detail in the Constitutions but not in the Codex, are the source of Opus Dei's tight control over its membership.) Former and active members have said they know nothing of the articles in the Constitutions.

Many devout people are members of Opus Dei. Dozens are convinced that by praying to Escrivá, who died in 1975, they have received miraculous help. But Opus is also an efficient machine, dominated by fundamentalist European priests, that seeks broader international influence. Although Opus disclaims this, insisting that its task is solely to guide members towards correct moral choices, there is a fatal duality in its scheme: while it pushes members to succeed as adults in the secular world, it treats them like children in religious matters. 'You need a director [a priest] in order to offer yourself, to surrender yourself

. . . by obedience', Escrivá told his followers. (He spoke to his recruits as the 'Nursery'.) Through weekly confession, 'heart-to-heart' talks, or 'confidences', and other contacts, members of Opus receive instruction on every aspect of their lives. On the one hand they are told, 'Obey and you will be saved', noted Father Pedro Miguel Lamet, former director of the Spanish religious weekly *Vida Nueva*. On the other, they are urged to succeed in a competitive world in order to attract new members and to defray Opus Dei's considerable financial costs. The conflict between child and adult often ends in rebellion against a 'religious prison', as one recruit described it, and explains why Opus has produced so many disillusioned former members.

Although onetime members say that Opus Dei gives more importance to the Father (Escrivá) than to the Pope, John Paul seems not to mind. He often praises the movement's dedication, and personally ordains its priests. He has also appointed Opus members to important positions. Joaquín Navarro-Vals, a Spanish adherent, was named Vatican press spokesman, and an Opus Dei priest became a top adviser to the powerful Congregation for the Doctrine of the Faith, the latter-day version of the Inquisition. The Work's priests and sympathizers have been appointed bishops in Latin America and Europe through the good offices of Bernardin Cardinal Gantin, head of the Congregation for Bishops and an Opus Dei sympathizer himself. The congregation's secretary, Archbishop Lucas Moreira Neves, who was later named Cardinal of São Salvador, Brazil, also looks favourably on Opus, as does Eduardo Cardinal Martínez Somalo of Spain, for many years the second highest official at the Secretariat of State.

Indicative of the damage that Opus Dei can inflict is the rapidly changing situation in Peru where, in addition to controlling a university, it counts seven bishops as members, one-ninth of the country's total. Birthplace of the theology of liberation, Peru in the early 1970s took the lead in encouraging religious support for popular empowerment, startling the Vatican with an endorsement of socialism. In the following decade the number of religious vocations shot up, and many of the young priests and nuns went to work in slums or impoverished villages to help the people organize. But after John Paul's election a cold wind began to blow over the Andes, and by 1985 all Peru's archdioceses were controlled by conservatives, save Lima, where the ageing Juan Cardinal Landázuri Ricketts held firm. But Landázuri is due to retire, and when he leaves it is unlikely that the few remaining progressives in the hierarchy will be able to withstand pressure from Rome to cease sponsorship of church work that empowers the poor. Landázuri's departure may also clear the way for a Vatican condemnation of the Peruvian priest Gustavo Gutiérrez, the father of liberation theology.

Latin America's economic elites and their allies in the United States and Europe have been seeking such sanctions for nearly a decade. Since 1980, when Reagan's Latin America advisers attacked liberation theology for challenging 'productive capitalism', it has frequently been denounced as a source of 'Communist' agitation among the masses, most recently at a regional conference of the chiefs of Latin America's armies. While it was the Bible, not Marx, that inspired the theology, progressive Catholic leaders have used it as an instrument to subvert the status quo by encouraging the poor to challenge unjust economic and political structures. Despite his frequent exhortations to respect human rights, the Pope frowns upon this activism because he senses a faintly Marxist odour about people who are fighting an anti-Communist establishment. The solution, he believes, is to give more power to groups like Opus Dei—hence its ascendancy in Peru, Chile, Brazil, and El Salvador, where progressive church leaders have been systematically replaced by right-wing papal 'yes men'.

Although Opus Dei does not enjoy the same influence in the United States, it cooperates with Legatus, a high-powered businessmen's group founded by Catholic millionaire Thomas Monaghan, owner of the Detroit Tigers, and with the Knights of Malta, whose US membership comprises a Who's Who of the Catholic Republican establishment. Both Legatus and the Knights of Malta have ties to a US variation of Opus called Word of God, which enjoys Vatican support, has links with the CIA and, like Opus, is active in Central America.

US church sources say the importance of such groups stems not from the size of their membership, which is relatively small, but from papal approval. While many US bishops are opposed to the secrecy, intrigue and elitism that characterize 'the movements', as they are known in Vatican parlance, others, particularly the more than 100 bishops appointed during John Paul's reign, are more susceptible to Vatican directives. Cardinal O'Connor, for example, has welcomed Opus Dei priests to the New York archdiocese, and Cardinal Law has frequently shown Opus favour, even travelling to Spain to ordain its priests. O'Connor and Law also favor Opus Dei campus ministries for universities in their areas, including Columbia, Harvard, and the Massachusetts Institute of Technology. Liberal bishops worry less about possible inroads by Opus—most students are turned off by its dogmatism—than about the portent of papal intentions. Were the US church to uphold John Paul's 'perfect society', it would not only deny its own history of respect for the separation of church and state but also risk being reduced to a marginal church similar to that of the Protestant fundamentalists. Yet the signs are not encouraging. Confrontations have become increasingly frequent, and ugly, between hard-line bishops and Catholic politicians who refuse to vote as Rome directs.

The subtleties of US political culture, which has traditionally balanced the tensions between religion and democracy, are beyond the grasp of a Vatican bureaucracy heavily weighted with Opus Dei advocates and a Pope reared in an East European tradition of 'Obey and be saved'. But as public opinion surveys show, most US Catholics are not about to obey, particularly in sexual matters. Nor do they believe it necessary to agree with the Pope in order to be good Catholics. They don't want his 'perfect society', and, the surveys suggest, the more it is forced on them, the more they react like Americans, not Roman Catholics.

*   *   *

Religious fundamentalists usually bring to mind well-known stereotypes—Jim and Tammy Bakker pleading poverty from their multimillion-dollar home or Pat Robertson ordering a hurricane to retreat. Yet fundamentalism is not limited to the Bible Belt, to a particular kind of Protestantism or to a single country, as shown by its upsurge in Iran and Israel. The most powerful fundamentalist of them all, at least in terms of the number of followers he commands, was not the Ayatollah Ruhollah Khomeini or an American evangelical but Pope John Paul II, leader of the Catholic world. A throwback to the 1950s, before the reforms undertaken by the Second Vatican Council (Vatican II), the Polish Pontiff has the same characteristics as those of Moslem, Jewish, and Protestant fundamentalists, including a reverence for authority and a fear of secularization—or 'secular humanism', as the Vatican and US evangelicals call it. Like his counterparts in other religions, John Paul insists that his church alone possesses the truth. 'To deserve the name at all', the Pope told a Polish audience, 'a civilization must be a Christian civilization'. He has also aligned himself with the political right, another characteristic of religious fundamentalists.

Although much was made of President Ronald Reagan's ties to Jerry Falwell and other Protestant fundamentalists, the Pope actually did more to further the Republican cause by disciplining Reagan's most outspoken Catholic critics and throwing the church's institutional weight behind groups identified with US interests, such as anti-Sandinista Catholics in Nicaragua. While John Paul has followed his own agenda, which is primarily concerned with re-establishing Vatican authority over local churches, Rome's interests have frequently coincided with those of the White House, producing a 'parallelism in viewpoints', to quote Archbishop Pio Laghi, the Vatican's Ambassador to the United States. At the same time, US Catholic fundamentalists played a key role in providing the church with the means to attack Reagan's domestic critics, such as the 'peace' bishops who in the early 1980s persuaded the Catholic hierarchy to write a pastoral letter that challenged Washington's nuclear arms build-up.

An important figure in the fundamentalist Catholic cause is Paul Weyrich, a founder of the New Right who was influential in advancing Falwell's career and who is credited with coining the phrase 'Moral Majority'. Weyrich also helped found the Heritage Foundation with the financial aid of Joseph Coors, the ultraconservative vice chair of the Coors brewery and an adviser to President Reagan. Heritage, the first and most influential of the New Right think tanks, was for several years directed by Frank Shakespeare, a friend of Reagan's and US Ambassador to the Vatican. Like John Paul, Weyrich is a pre-Vatican II Catholic who wants to resurrect a religion based on absolutism and infallible certitudes. He objected to the bishops' discussing the nuclear arms issue, which was not, he said, a proper subject for religious consideration. Nor did he agree with liturgical and other reforms in church ritual and administration. Working with the archconservative Minnesota-based newspaper *The Wanderer*, Catholics United for the Faith, and other fundamentalist groups, Weyrich encouraged US Catholics to complain to Rome about such activists as Seattle's Archbishop Raymond Hunthausen, who supported the Sanctuary movement and opposed US arms policies. To teach Catholics how to turn the screws, Weyrich organized the Washington-based Catholic Center, which sent 'truth squads' backed by Coors money to organize workshops in Seattle and other cities with progressive bishops. But the emphasis was always on the religious not the political side: Hunthausen and others like him had scandalized the faithful by allowing homosexuals to sponsor masses—they were poisoning the minds of the flock; they were destroying the church. Weyrich stressed the importance of 'labelling the opposition, putting them in a box and telling others that the opposition is composed of people who do not follow the Pope'.

The tactic paid off because John Paul's papacy is 'constitutionally disposed', in the words of an American Jesuit with long experience in Rome, to believe such smears. Because of their respect for pluralism and an openness to dialogue and innovation, the American bishops are viewed as 'unruly' by the Curia Romana—in other words, they have not copied the Polish model of Catholicism, in which everyone follows the leader and no one dares dissent. Sharing John Paul's distrust of democracy (of which he has had no experience), the Curia assumed that the truth squads' accusations were correct without checking the facts (a common Vatican practice, according to many bishops).

In 1986, Hunthausen, who had been singled out for abuse by Weyrich, *The Wanderer* and other Catholic fundamentalists, was stripped of many of his powers, although the charges against him were untrue or exaggerated, or were common practice in US churches, such as providing religious services for homosexuals. Bishop Walter Sullivan of Richmond, Virginia, also a peace activist and likewise humiliated by Vatican disciplining, said publicly what many US prelates privately admitted—that Hunthausen's punishment 'on ecclesiastical issues' made no sense unless it was related to the peace question, since many other dioceses followed similar religious practices. Hunthausen did not preside over a politically powerful see with millions of Catholics, nor was Seattle important to the Vatican's finances, compared with, say, Chicago or New York. His ecclesiastical positions made him vulnerable to Vatican discipline, and his stand on the nuclear issue assured that any moves the Vatican made against him would be endorsed in the United States by right-wing Catholics and powerful political and business interests—including the Federal Bureau of Investigation, which had kept files on Hunthausen's antiwar activities.

A stream of important US officials had visited the Vatican in the early 1980s, including President Reagan, Vice President George Bush, Secretary of State George Shultz, Defense Secretary Casper Weinberger, and retired Gen. Vernon Walters, former deputy director of the Central Intelligence Agency and at the time Reagan's roving ambassador. All or some may have questioned the bishops' pastoral letter in nuclear arms, which had caused considerable handwringing in the White House. In any case, Rome, by punishing Hunthausen, sent a warning to the US bishops to pay more attention to spiritual matters and less to political ones, and at the same time gave the White House symbolic support in the controversy over the arms race. The Pope made a similar point on his visit to the United States in 1987 by ignoring the bishops' pastoral letter despite its historic significance. Edward Rowny, White House special adviser on arms control, could thus state that the Reagan Administration's defence policies were 'in harmony' with the Pope's criteria but not with some positions adopted by the US bishops.

John Paul proved equally helpful in Nicaragua by supporting Sandinista critics and thus furthering the *Contra* cause. Not until the end of Reagan's second term did Vatican officials privately admit that it had been a mistake to depend on Washington to solve the church's problems in Nicaragua. Like the Reagan Administration, the Vatican believed Nicaragua was setting a bad example for the rest of Latin America. Not only had the Nicaraguans thrown off the gringo yoke; they were refusing to take orders from Rome. The spectre of religion-fuelled rebellion worried both power centres, which saw liberation theology as the wedge for Marxist revolution. In fact, most of the region's liberation theologies are not Marxist, but neither Washington nor Rome was inclined to waste time trying to distinguish one theology from another. One had only to look at Nicaragua, said the State Department and the Curia, to know what could happen elsewhere in Latin America.

In late 1986, when it had become clear that Washington would not succeed in overthrowing the Sandinistas, the Vatican belatedly initiated overtures to the revolutionary government. But while negotiations helped reduce tensions between church and state, John Paul remained convinced that Nicaragua would go the way of Poland. The Nicaraguan hierarchy refused to condemn the *Contras*, and Managua's Cardinal, Miguel Obando y Bravo, actively continued to take their part.

Obando, who in 1985 was singled out for papal favour by becoming Central America's only cardinal, was the principal contact in the region for a network of right-wing religious organizations that have gained prominence during John Paul's reign. Sharing an elitist world view and fundamentalist religious convictions, these groups have often worked together to achieve the Vatican's—and Washington's—objectives in Central America. They include:

- Opus Dei, a fundamentalist lay movement founded in Spain and favoured by the Pope;
- Communion and Liberation (CL), a more modern, Italian version of Opus that also enjoys papal support;
- Knights of Malta, a 900-year-old chivalric order, members of which are drawn from the European aristocracy and the upper classes in North and South America;
- Legatus, a Catholic club for American Executives at companies earning more than $4 million annually;
- Word of God, a US variation of Opus Dei and CL, and its international affiliate, Sword of the Spirit;
- The Institute on Religion and Democracy (IRD), a neoconservative group founded during Reagan's first term and dubbed 'the official seminary of the White House' by its critics.

First on the scene in Nicaragua was Sword of the Spirit, which established a group in Managua in 1978, a year before the Sandinistas toppled the Somoza dictatorship. Its affiliate, Word of God, formed part of the fundamentalist Catholic revival in the United States in the 1960s, later evolving into a highly structured organization in which 'shepherds' control all aspects of members' lives, much as Opus Dei does. Headquartered in Ann Arbor, Michigan, it has branches in various parts of the United States and works closely with the fundamentalist Franciscan University of Steubenville, in Ohio. Sword of the Spirit is active in several world hot spots, including the Philippines and South Africa. The Managua branch, which was formed by wealthy businessmen with the support of Cardinal Obando, soon attracted a Who's Who of Sandinista opponents. Internal Sword of the Spirit documents obtained by Michigan journalist Russ Bellant show that the aim of the group was to mobilize religious and political opposition to the revolutionary government. According to the documents, the Pope was to play a central part in stirring up Catholics during his visit to Nicaragua in 1983—

a role he fulfilled, albeit with largely negative results, by shouting down Sandinista supporters during a huge open-air mass in Managua.

Among the Sword of the Spirit's recruits was Humberto Belli, an editor of the opposition *La Prensa* and a trusted associate of Obando, who was responsible for Belli's appointment in 1982 as a consultant to the Vatican Secretariat for Non-Believers. By that time Belli was also working with the IRD, board members of which included Catholic writer Michael Novak and Lutheran pastor Richard John Neuhaus. The IRD's goal was to gain religious support for Reagan's foreign policies, particularly in Central America. Belli was among several 'stars' promoted by the institute in its campaign to portray the Sandinistas as godless Communists. Also part of the campaign, and closely associated with the IRD, were Friends of the Democratic Center in Central America (Prodemca), which funnelled US government funds to the Nicaraguan opposition, and the James Madison Foundation, another neoconservative Catholic think tank. The foundation is headed by George Weigel, an academic version of Novak, and supported by Jeane Kirkpatrick's husband, Evron. Weigel is also a board member of the IRD and the Puebla Institute. The latter was founded in Michigan in 1982 as a vehicle to distribute Belli's first book, *Nicaragua: Christians Under Fire*, which, according to former *Contra* leader Edgar Chamorro, was conceived and funded by the CIA. Puebla's first directors were Word of God members, and it was through Word of God that Belli became an associate professor of sociology at the Franciscan University of Steubenville.

One of Word of God's most important backers is Michigan millionaire Thomas Monaghan, a fast-food entrepreneur, owner of the Detroit Tigers and a member of the board of trustees of the Franciscan University of Steubenville. Monaghan is also the founder of Legatus, the highpowered Catholic businessmen's club that has Vatican support and has attracted such influential millionaires as Lewis Lehrman, whose drugstore-chain fortune made him the moneybag of the New York Republican Party after Nelson Rockefeller's death; William Simon, Treasury Secretary under Richard Nixon and Gerald Ford; and J. Peter Grace, head of the petrochemical giant W. R. Grace. Legatus's director, Marlene Elwell, was co-chair of the Michigan campaign for the Bush–Quayle ticket and, earlier, Midwest director for Pat Robertson's presidential campaign. Also a familiar figure in Legatus circles is the ubiquitous Paul Weyrich, which is not surprising in view of the organization's pet hates—secular humanism and liberation theology—which have frequently come under attack by Weyrich's fundamentalist followers.

Legatus's principal overseas interest is Honduras, head-quarters of the *Contras* and also a religious target of such Prot-estant fundamentalists as Pat Robertson and Jimmy Swaggart. Among the groups working with Legatus there are the local branches of Sword of the Spirit and Opus Dei. Honduras is also much favoured by the Knights of Malta, which channelled millions of dollars in supplies to the *Contra* camps. Distribution was facilitated by the Knights' diplomatic privileges (the organi-zation claims to be a sovereign state) and its Central American members, particularly Roberto Alejos, a wealthy Guatemalan sugar and coffee grower. The Knights' ambassador to Honduras, Alejos has had a relationship with the CIA since 1960, when the agency used his estates to train Cubans for the Bay of Pigs invasion. Among the main promoters of such funding were for-mer Treasury Secretary Simon, a Knight, and Grace, head of the American Association of the Knights.

Last January, following initiation ceremonies for new Knights and Dames at St. Patrick's Cathedral in New York City, Presi-dent Reagan was given the order's Collar of the Order of Merit 'for his vigorous defence of the pro-life cause, and his strong support of traditional Christian family values'. Among the new Knights present for the occasion were Monaghan and Ralph Martin, co-founder of Word of God.

On the surface, the activities of such groups seem concerned primarily with spreading the gospel of corporate business and helping Washington counter such subversive influences as the Sandinistas. More is involved, however, because the network has direct lines to the Vatican and the blessing of a fundamentalist Pope who exercises considerable power, particularly in predominantly Catholic regions like Central America. Another group the Pope relies on to spread his fundamentalist message is Communion and Liberation, a militant Italian Catholic movement that has gained infuence in the right wing of the Christian Democrats and is a strong political force in northern Italy, particularly Milan. According to Stanislaw Grygiel, a Polish professor brought to Rome by John Paul and who forms part of his Polish court, CL, Opus Dei, and other such movements will provide the dedicated troops the Pope needs to refashion the Catholic Church in his own, fundamentalist image. Grygiel himself has carried that vision to the Franciscan University of Steubenville, where he has lectured with word of God founder Martin and with Humberto Belli. Word of God has also developed links with CL sponsors in the Curia, such as Bishop Paul Cordes, vice president of the Pontifical council of the Laity, and Edouard Cardinal Gagnon, president of the Pontifical Council for the Family. Gagnon claims the Pope is about to add Word of God to his most favoured list. The movement also has the support of Bernard Cardinal Law of Boston, a papal loyalist and, with New York City's John Cardinal O'Connor, the leader of the fundamentalist resurgence in the US Catholic Church. (Both men are prominent members of the Knights of Malta and strong supporters of Cardinal Obando y Bravo.)

Although the IRD has long had direct lines of communication with the Vatican and CL through Michael Novak and George Weigel, the Steubenville–Word of God connection indicates that the Vatican is moving beyond small circles of intellectuals to develop a larger base of right-wing lay movements with financial and political clout in order to pursue John Paul's geopolitical vision. Nicaragua remains a crucial element in the strategy because, unlike Cuba, it symbolizes Christian–Marxist cooperation in the world's most populous Catholic region. Some high-ranking Sandinista officials believe that the religious question could in the long run cause the government more damage than the *Contras* inflicted, because it involves churches that affect Nicaraguan attitudes towards the Sandinistas and the government's image abroad.

Although the Vatican is willing to pretend neutrality as the price for maintaining a space in revolutionary Nicaragua, John Paul is as vehemently opposed to the Sandinistas as was President Reagan. Religious pressures will therefore continue. While the Pope possesses no divisions, as Stalin once sneered, he has in the emerging network of fundamentalist groups a formidable weapon that can funnel resources to Obando's church and, more important, keep up political pressure to isolate Nicaragua as an international pariah. President Bush may be more pragmatic in dealing with the Sandinistas—seeing will be believing—but if so, he will have to contend with a powerful religious lobby, including the Knights of Malta, which forms part of his own East Coast establishment.

Towards the end of Reagan's Administration officials of the Curia Romana took to ridiculing the 'cowboy' President because of his crude power plays. Yet John Paul shares several characteristics with the former President, including a love of the theatrical and a mental fixity about the past. The main difference is that while Reagan's convictions are superficial, like the celluloid characters he once portrayed, the Pope's beliefs are deep-rooted, passionate and unmarred by doubt—the mark of the true fundamentalist.

The Riddle of the Middle East: Religion or Geopolitics?

Georges Corm*

Thanks to the image presented in the media, in the press, and in popular literature, the average European observer sees the conflicts in the Middle East as conflicts motivated by religious divisions, fanaticism, backwardness, and even barbarism. In order to gain a fairer view of the situation, it is necessary to reject racial stereotypes and search more carefully for the truth, but the social realities of the Middle East are so complex that Europeans have great difficulty understanding the conflicts and what is behind them. 'Informed' politicians tend to say that it is beyond Europe's capacities to intervene in the conflicts and that only a major power like the USA can contain and manage the conflicts in the best interests of the Western bloc.

We never hear nowadays of the role played by Europe in the Middle East from the Renaissance to the colonial era which ended just a few decades ago. Of the history of the Middle East, the diversity of its society and culture, the rapid pace of socio-economic development since the end of the nineteenth century, we hear nothing, apart from pseudo-academic and media discussions on Islam fundamentalism. The endless monotony of these discussions is sometimes enlivened by minor excursions into the differences between 'Sunnis' and 'Shi'ites', but more often by an examination of the problems caused by the abun-

---

* Sociologist and historian of the contemporary Middle East, author of *Le Proche-Orient éclaté* (Paris, La Découverte, 1986), *Géopolitique du conflit libanais* (La Découverte, 1986) and *L'Europe et l'Orient: De la balkanisation à la libanisation* (La Découverte, 1989).

dance of religious or ethnic groupings in the Middle East: the Lebanese Maronites, the Druzes, the Alawites (a group to which the Syrian head of state belongs), the Kurds scattered between Iraq, Iran, Turkey, the Copts of Egypt, and so on.

Thus, religious references have come to dominate European discourse on the Middle East. In particular, it is perhaps the Lebanese conflict which has given rise to the most prolific use of exclusively religious language. Lebanon itself—its society, its people, its state which has struggled for life for the last fourteen years—remains unknown and does not impinge on the debate. European observers and politicians see only religious groupings and their military leaders: a Christian 'enclave' and pro-Syrain 'Muslims'.

Nowhere in these discussions does the remarkable story of Mount Lebanon appear; here, Druze, Maronite, and Shi'ite communities intermingled for centries and created a dense network of human and economic relations with the historic coastal towns (Beirut, Sidon, Tyre, Tripoli with its Sunni and Greek orthodox population). Nowhere do we hear of the open and liberal Lebanese society before 1975. Neither do we hear of the intensive bombardment which began on New Year's Eve 1968 with the spectacular attack on Beirut airport which so angered General de Gaulle. Israeli attacks, aimed at preventing the use of Lebanon as a base for armed Palestinian action against Israeli territory, have continued ever since, even after invasions of Lebanon by Israel in 1978 and 1982. Nowhere do we see mention of the various wars waged by many different groups (Falangists, Israelis, Syrians, Amal 'Shi'ite' militia) against the Palestinian camps in Lebanon: Tal al Zaatar in 1976, Sabra-Chatila in 1982, Beirut, Saïda and Tyre between 1985 and 1988.

Religious categorizations began to dominate discussion on Lebanon in 1975. There was talk of 'Christian conservatives' and 'Muslim progressives' or of a 'Palestinian-progressive coalition' or 'Muslim-progressive coalition'. Such terms are of course reductionist; they obscure reality and confine human action within stereotypes, thus preventing rational responses.

In fact, obscurantist use of religious vocabulary goes back to the creation of the 'Jewish' state of Israel in Palestine in 1948, the fruit of the mystic, Messianic political doctrine of Zionism which grew up in the Middle East, thanks to European antisemitism, the pogroms of Russia and Central Europe, and the Holocaust. The 'Hebrew' state was democratic from the point of view of the new Jewish society in Palestine, but not for those Palestinians who resisted fear and stayed in the territory of the new state. The Israeli state built a virtually impenetrable wall between 'Jews' and Palestinian Arabs (whether Christian or Muslim).

In 1948, the Middle East had no 'Muslim' states (except for the very specific case of Wahabism[1] in Saudi Arabia) like Pakistan, which came into being around that time amidst great bloodshed, as a result of the secession from the Indian empire of part of the Muslim population who did not wish to live under the domination of the Brahmin majority in a newly independent India. Few people seem to know that Middle Eastern societies have been pluralistic from the earliest times. None of the empires which ruled the area until the end of the First World War forced the populations to lose their pluralism. Neither European-style cultural and linguistic homogenization nor industrialization affected the communities of the Middle East in this way. Admittedly, the Arab states emerging from the disintegration of the Ottoman empire were to follow the path towards national unification, but they did not seek to impose Islam as the unifying

[1] Wahabism is an Islamic puritan doctrine founded by Mr. Abdelwahab at the beginning of the eighteenth century. The Saudi family used Wahabism in its attempts during the eighteenth and nineteenth century to create a Bedouin state, tinged with an aggressive political mysticism, in the heart of the Arab peninsula. Because of this, the Wahabi doctrine was fiercely opposed by Sunni Muslims in all the major centres of the Middle East. It was not until the twentieth century that the Saudi project succeeded, thanks to the historical situation created by the end of the First World War, the disintegration of the Ottoman empire and English colonial policy in the Middle East. On Wahabism and the foundation of the Saudi kingdom, see the outstanding work by Y. Besson, *Ibn Sa'oud, Roi bédouin, La naissance du Royaume d'Arabie Séoudite* (Lausanne, Edition des Trois Continents, 1980) And an enlightening article by the same author, 'L'Ikhwan d'Ibn S'aoud: mouvement national?' in *Guerres modernes,*, no. 153/1989.

factor; traditions of religious tolerance were too strong in the
Arab states of the East. Although Islam was declared the state
religion, there was no religious persecution, no 'ghettos' in the
towns.[1] Secularism, already important in the nineteenth century,
spread and developed in the twentieth century. It is noteworthy
that when the newly independent Arab states gathered together
in solidarity at the end of the First World War, they did not
call their organization the Islamic League or the Arab Islamic
League, but the Arab League.

The ideologies which dominated the 1950s and 1960s—Nas-
serism and Baath—were nationalist and securalist, seeking to
unite and to overcome socio-geographical differences. Religion
appeared only marginally in discourse on identity or national
allegiance. Israel was opposed not as a Jewish state but as the
colonial occupier of a state which had been part of the Arab
world since the seventh century. Had it been Buddhists or
Christians who had settled in Palestine and built a state at the
expense of the native Palestians, the reaction would have been
the same. Arabs could not see why the Middle East should pay
the price for the persecution and extermination of Jews in
Europe.

Their reaction was understandable given that pluralistic
Middle East society has a long tradition of taking in and shelter-
ing Jews: Jews of Arab descent, Sephardic Jews fleeing from the
Spanish *Reconquista*. The modern state which Israel embodied,
based on a single religion, was seen in the Middle East as an
unnatural phenomenon and a potential threat to pluralist societies. The construction of European-style modern states in the
Middle East, on the other hand, called for uniformity not on the
basis of religion but on the basis of shared language and culture.
Quite simply, there is too much religious diversity to envisage
homogenization: as well as the numerous Arabized Eastern

[1] General Pierre Rondot has written dispassionately and perceptively on
the question of minorities in the Near East in two remarkable articles which
have appeared recently: 'Les minorités dans le Proche-Orient' in *L'Afrique et
l'Asie moderne* no. 151/Winter 1986–1987, no. 152/Spring 1978 (CHEAM,
Paris).

Christian Churches, there are also the various unorthodox and esoteric Muslim sects, such as the Druzes, the Alawites, the Ismailis, the Abadites, and the Shi'ite Muslims whose religious beliefs are different from those of the majority Sunnis. The pre-occupation of the Arab states was therefore not religious but cultural homogenization: cultural minorities also exist, notably the Kurds, the Turkmen, and the Circassians, which belong mainly to Sunni Islam but which do not share the Arabic language or culture; similarly, problems of cultural integration occurred with the influx of Armenian refugees from the Turkish massacres around the turn of the century.

The creation of the state of Israel created fertile ground for tensions and conflicts, exacerbated by the struggle between the superpowers for control of the Middle East, strategically important because of its geographical position and its energy resources. Conflicts were further fuelled by the leadership struggle between the Arab states. The conjunction of these three factors helps to explain the extreme political instability in the Arab world in the 1950s and 1960s. A new generation of republican, secularist officers replaced the older, aristocratic or bourgeois ruling classes. The young officers now looked to the example of the Young Turks and the creation of a strong, modern, secularist state by Mustapha Kemel: in other words, to the Turkish nationalism, inspired by the French revolution, which had, in conjunction with the struggle between the European powers for parts of the disintegrating Ottoman empire, resulted in the genocide of the Armenians, the persecution of the Kurds, and the break between Turks and Arabs which occurred at the beginning of the nineteenth century. Following this example, a wave of secularist republicanism swept across Egypt, Iraq, and the Yemen, toppling the monarchies of those countries despite their religious legitimation.[1]

The Arab republics' campaign against the state of Israel was not built on a religious mobilization. On the contrary, the 1960s

[1] On this, see Georges Corm, 'Les coups d'Etat au Moyen-Orient', *Les coups d'Etat* (Etudes Polémologiques) no. 41/Spring 1987 (French Institute of War Studies, Paris).

saw the rise of pro-Soviet or pro-Chinese radicalism as the biggest ideological factor supporting the emergence of the PLO as the coordinator of guerrilla movements fighting against the usurpation of Palestinian land, for the right to return to the land taken over by Israel in 1948 and for the withdrawal of Israeli troops from the territories occupied after the war of June 1967.

In the Middle East, only the minority, right-wing Muslim Brotherhood referred to Islam as the vector of political and social reconstruction. For the Muslim Brotherhood, the victorious Israeli state, built on a single religion, exemplified the power and force of religious resurgence; the Jewish experience in Europe and the democratic functioning of the Israeli state within the Jewish community, on the other hand, lay outside their knowledge and understanding. Between 1950 and 1970, the Muslim Brotherhood was banned from political life and often forcibly suppressed, as in Egypt. Later, however, a series of events occurred which encouraged the revival of the movement and thus helped to hide the real meaning of the Middle East conflict under the veil of Islam.

The events which caused Islam to become the central political reference in the Middle East were the oil crisis of the 1970s and the tough American response to the rapid extension of Soviet influence in the Middle East, Africa, and Asia. If the West was to feel the effects of these developments in the 1980s, the Third World was immediately and profoundly shaken by them. Saudi Arabia was then the only Arab state based on religious fundamentalism, in the form of the Wahabi doctrine. The country and its doctrine (until then marginal in the Arab world) now assumed a major importance thanks to its rich oil reserves. Moreover, it suited the USA, protector of Saudi Arabia, to encourage Wahabism in order to combat the Marxist influences then spreading in the under-developed countries: Nasserite or Baathist radicalism in the Arab league, the non-aligned movement which was moving dangerously close to Moscow, the Three Worlds theory, Guevarists and other Marxist or progressive doctrines.

'Islam' was thus seen as a convenient and effective weapon against Marxism, backed up by the financial strength of the oil

producers. Fundamentalist Islam was as much opposed to the
Marxist atheism embodied in the USSR as to the idea of cultural
communities or ethnic specificities, preferring instead the millenarianist[1] utopia of the reign of 'the city of God' and the
fulfilment of holy law. Thus encouraged, the spread of Muslim
fundamentalism took various forms, from the financial pressure
exerted in many African countries, to the Islamic coup which
brought President Zia to power in Pakistan.

Even President Sadat had a hand in this process. He was close
to the Saudis and hoped to use the Muslim Brotherhood to
reduce the influence of the democratic socialist students' movement in Egypt. He dissolved the Nasserite youth organizations
in all the Egyptian universities and replaced them with the very
groups of Muslim Brothers his predecessor had banned from
politics; he also allowed some Muslim Brothers to stand in parliamentary elections and demand the restoration of the *Shari'a*
(the Islamic holy law, which had been in force prior to the move
towards European modernization in the eighteenth century, but
which had been applied with varying degrees of rigour according
to the time, the ruler, and the interpretations given by the various
schools of thought and legal traditions). The freedom given to
the Muslim Brotherhood resulted in the most violent clashes for
centuries between Egyptian Christians (Copts) and Muslims in
the poorer urban and rural centres. Sadat finally fell victim to
his own political manoeuvring: he was killed by supporters of a
millenarianist Muslim sect (an offshoot of the Muslim Brotherhood) whose formation his Islamic revival had encouraged.

In the Sudan, President Numeiry went even further than Sadat
in bowing to the influence of US-Saudi oil money. His decision

[1] The term 'millenarianism' is used here to underline the relationship
between forms of Muslim fundamentalism which occur among the marginalized social classes, and Jewish and Christian millenarianist traditions. These
traditions are well described in N. Cohen, *Les fanatiques de l'Apocalypse,
pseudo-messies prophètes et illuminés du Moyen Age* (Julliard, Paris, 1957).
The striking resemblance between Judaeo-Christian and Islam millenarianism stems from the Koran's constant references to the Old Testament.
Indeed, it is all too often forgotten that Islam, like Christianity, sees itself as
the continuation of Judaic monotheism.

to impose application of the *Shari'a* reawakened the civil war with animists and Christians in southern Sudan, which he had courageously appeased only a few years earlier.

Around the same time, a rival organization to the Arab League and the non-aligned movement was set up under Saudi and Pakistani leadership. The Conference of Islamic States, founded in Mecca in 1969, represented more than fifty African and Asian states, but it was not until the mid-1970s that it expanded and consolidated its activities on the international scene, thanks to the oil resources which enabled the Muslim states of the Third World to further their political ambitions under the banner of Islam. In 1974, the Islamic Development Bank was established in Jeddah with the aim of financing the development of the countries belonging to the Conference, according to the principles of the *Shari'a*. In addition, private oil revenue financed the creation of an extensive network of Islamic banks and financial institutions in Africa and Asia; a number of scandals were to rock these new channels of 'Islamic' influence, notably in Egypt in 1988, when hundreds of small savers lost the few pounds they had managed to save. Meanwhile, religious charities were busy giving grants to those families willing to convert to the new forms of Islamic puritanism (for instance, to women who would wear the veil). Oil dollars soon became 'Islam dollars' as American and Saudi oil money financed the transformation of the Arab states.

In this changed atmosphere, the Palestinian conflict began to take on the appearance of a war between Islam and Judaism. In reality, however, the political objectives of the Arab states were not primarily religious. After the Russian invasion of Afghanistan in 1979, the Conference of Islamic States concentrated on denouncing Russian expansionism and the Soviet union in general, then on the Iran–Iraq war which set two 'Islamic' nations against each other.

In order to understand this conflict it is necessary to go back to the Iranian revolution, which was quickly taken over by the religious 'soviets' led by Khomeini from his refuge in France. For months, and with the evident indulgence of politicians and the media in the West, Khomeini outdid the popular agitation aroused by the nationalist and Marxist-inspired organizations hostile to the Shah. Outdoing Lenin (who returned in an armoured train to Russia through German territory and with the full knowledge of the German authorities), Khomeini went back to Iran with all the honours of a head of state, in a Boeing 747 charted by the French government—which in fact recognized the Shah's regime. It was thought at this stage that the fanatical Khomeini would become a key part of the Saudi-led, pro-Western Islamic network; like the West, revolutionary Iran too had to face the threat of Soviet Marxism. Indeed, as expected, Khomeini's regime led a hunt against Marxists and secularist nationalists. But the West did not reckon on the primary anti-Westernism which allowed Khomeini to eliminate all opponents and to maintain the implacable dictatorship of the clergy over fifty million Iranians. The West received its first lesson with the episode of the American hostages in Tehran.

Outflanking the conservative, pro-Western proponents of 'state Islam' in the Conference of Islamic States, the Khomeini regime next sought to extend its domination of the Arab Middle East (the Shah's old dream) by imposing a new, militant Shi'ite theology which broke with the traditional quietism of Shi'a, so well described in the works of Henri Corbin.[1] The new regime used various weapons to achieve this aim: the mobilization of Shi'ite Arabs against Sunnis, the suppression of even the most basic form of social pluralism and secularist behaviour in the Middle East, the increasing number of attempted 'Islamic' coups in the Arab states, and the PLO struggle against the state of Israel.

Secular, Baathist Iraq became the first target of this policy because half its population was Shi'ite. Iran formed a solid alliance with the Syrian regime of Hafez Assad, which left Iraq

[1] Corbin's monumental work on this subject, especially his *Histoire de la philosophie islamique* (Paris, Gallimard, 1964), like the invaluable research of Massignon, Berque, Rodinson, Colombe, and others, is unfortunately neglected today in France and Europe in favour of works preoccupied solely with 'Islamic fundamentalism', a deviation that is wrongly presented as the true representation of the psyche of the 'Muslim people'.

isolated. The alliance was motivated by tactical reasons which
had nothing to do with religious solidarity; on the contrary, the
Syrian regime itself, led by a member of the minority, unorthodox Alawite sect, was secular and had brutally put down the
insurrectionary Muslim Brotherhood, for instance in Hama in
1981. The Syrian alliance gave Iran a strategic bridgehead in
Lebanon. Wishing to get rid of the American and French contin-
gents of the peacekeeping force in Lebanon, Syria offered Iran
the chance to send units of the Revolutionary Guards to
Lebanon to organize the training of the Party of God (Hezbollah) and various Islamic Holy War (Jehad) groups responsible
for hostage-taking in Beirut. Iran's power over the West was
thus boosted enormously. The 'Irangate' scandal revealed the
scale of American arms supplies to the Khomeini regime and
of the contacts between the US administration and the Iran
government financing hostage-taking in Lebanon. Even more
surprising were the revelations that the Israelis had acted as go-
between in these contacts, which the Israeli government portrayed as part of its general policy of dividing and weakening the
Arab states.

   If the Syrians actively helped to establish an Iranian presence
in Lebanon between 1982 and 1985, the Israeli army, which
occupied the whole of south Lebanon during this period, and
whose troops surrounded Beirut until 1983 (particularly the
famous southern part of the city where the Hezbollah was
entrenched), did nothing to prevent it. Israelis and Hezbollah
alike waged war against the numerous secularists, socialists, and
Pan-Arab nationalists within the Shi'ite community, and many
respected Lebanese intellectuals lost their life as a result. The
secularist, revolutionary, socialist climate which had prevailed
within the Shi'ite community in the 1960s and 1970s gave way
to a pro-Khomeini reign of terror. Men had to grow beards,
women to wear veils. Thanks to Iranian money, which also
financed hospitals, clinics, and schools, the Hezbollah soldiers
were the highest-paid of all the Lebanese militia-men. The presence of the Western media from Baalbek to Tyre and even in
the southern part of Beirut ensured that these developments

received international attention, and created the illusion of an authentic and spontaneous 'Shi'ite' fanaticism.

Incidentally, these moves recalled the earlier intervention of Iran in Lebanon in the mid-sixties, when Imam Musa Sadir went to Lebanon, at the request of the Lebanese state, to try to stop the spread of Arab socialist nationalism among the increasingly radical youth of the country, by stimulating and organizing a religious revival in the Shi'ite community.

Among the Lebanese Christians, the Falangist party has played a parallel role since the end of the 1960s. With only five of the fifty-five Christian deputies in the Lebanese parliament (out of the total of ninety-nine), in 1975, the Falangist party began a campaign aimed at the destruction of the Lebanese state in order to gain total control of what the Falangist militia (the 'Lebanese Forces') call 'Christian society'. In fact, its campaign forced the mass expulsion from its territory, not only of Lebanese Muslims, but also of secularist, socialist, and Pan-Arab Christians. Its alliances within the Arab world were unstable and it relied heavily on Israel for the training of its soldiers on Israeli territory by the Israeli secret service. The Falange cried out its fear of Islam and accused the West of betraying and abandoning its Christian brothers. In response, France and the US made the fatal mistake of using the Israeli invasion of 1982 as an opportunity to put the Falange into power, arguing that it would be able to rebuild a stable state in Lebanon. The tragic results of this decision for Lebanon and for the West are well-known: the assassination of Bashir Gemayel; the massacres of Sabra and Chatila; the election of Amin Gemayel, who then allowed the state to be sacked and plundered by the militias; the mass killings and forced resettlement of the people of the Chouf (Israel's role in this, as occupier of the territory, has yet to be fully exposed); lastly, the attacks on the multinational force, followed by the return in strength of Syria and the Palestinians, and the arrival on the scene of Iran.

*   *   *

This brief look at the recent history of the Middle East has shown that the motives behind the Middle East conflicts are not religious. They are struggles for power and ascendancy. Religious classifications are used systematically as a screen to hide reality, blur vision, and prevent the formulation of a realistic, coherent policy in the West. However, a change in attitudes is possible. The Soviet Union, currently preoccupied with its own *perestroika*, has begun to loosen its grip on the Middle East and Asia. This opens up the possibility of a change in US policy towards the Middle East. Europe also has a role to play, since it is undoubtedly in Europe's interest to ensure peace in the Mediterranean basin. Moreover, the relationship between the European states and their thousands of North African, Asian, and Turkish immigrants (lumped together under the 'Muslim' label) is also at stake: the Western media's unhealthy obsession with Islam serves only to destabilize immigrant communities, which have, as well as their religious allegiances, an attachment to the democratic, secular traditions of Europe.

Of course, the formulation of a realistic Middle East policy on the part of the West presupposes certain changes of attitude and behaviour. In particular, the Western powers would have to be rigorous in their application of the international laws which they have done so much to establish. The law must be upheld in all circumstances if stability is to return to the Middle East. In the United Nations, for instance, countries must learn to apply decisions and to exert maximum pressure on other countries to do the same. All too often, decisions are taken as an immediate response to urgent situations, without much thought for their application. The numerous UN resolutions on the Palestinian conflict, for instance, serve as examples of the way in which decisions are often reached but not implemented: the UN has passed resolutions affirming the right of Palestinian refugees to return to their homeland, and calling on Israel to withdraw from the territories occupied since 1967 and from the south of Lebanon (part of which has been occupied since 1978).

Europeans see the state of Israel as legitimate because of the violation of basic human rights and human dignity which the

Jews have endured throughout their history. But does the Jews' historical suffering place the Israeli state above the laws of the international community? In that case, what confidence can the Middle East have in the values proclaimed by the Western democracies? Using Israel as an example, Iran, Syria, and Libya can all claim that they too are above international law, and the international community will have to accept this. As a result, the law, which is the only real basis for collective security, loses its value, and priority is given instead to individual 'security requirements' which undermine collective security. Lebanon, for example, is no longer regarded as a society, a country, a state, nor even as the focus for an affirmation of a Palestinian identity, but has to bear the brunt of the security requirements of the regional powers.

How much more convenient it is to hide behind the emotive discourse of religion. As the 'Irangate' transactions showed, Americans and Iranians are in fact willing to trade off the Bible and the Koran in order to further their own geo-political interests. The international media are not above paying the local militia-men to pose as religious devotees in order to get their shots of Islamic zeal in the Shi'ite mosques of Lebanon or Iran. Similarly, Salman Rushdie's book became the pretext for setting off an unhealthy wave of unrest and was blown up into an affair of state. And when General Aoun (a general in the Lebanese army) resolved to liberate his country from both Israeli and Syrian occupation, he was dismissed as the 'leader of the Christian enclave' by the Western media, which preferred to speak of the 'legitimate interests' of Syria in Lebanon.

Democratic Europe, whose past is closely bound up with the origins of the Middle East conflicts, must help to restore respect for modern international law. As long as international law is flouted in the Middle East, Islamic millenarianism will continue to flourish, financed by states which are direct clients of the USA. The Middle East will remain a free-for-all, giving succour to bloody dictatorships and allowing the state of Israel to deny the existence of the Palestinian people and to attack the Lebanese people who have given them shelter.

It should not be forgotten that the Middle East remains the largest market for arms in the world and that the democratic and totalitarian states alike profit from it. The fear of unemployment caused by a decline in arms sales should not deter Europe from seeking other solutions. Just think of the boom in civilian trade which peace in the Middle East could bring to other European industries. The thousands of millions of ECU spent each year on arms could go into productive investment and create jobs for the thousands of young people who face unemployment in Europe and the Middle East today. This strategy alone could stamp out 'Islamic fundamentalism', but unfortunately it has few supporters among the ruling and intellectual circles in the East or in the West.

Religion and the Asian and Caribbean Minorities in Britain

Harry Goulbourne and Danièle Joly*

The religious dimension of the lives of people from South-east Asia and the Caribbean who have settled in Britain is being increasingly recognized as one of several changing aspects of post-War British society. The furore over Salman Rushdie's *Satanic Verses* during the past fifteen months or so, has served to highlight this fact. But at one point or another over the past forty years, religious belief and practice have been of grave concern to all minorities which have settled in a predominantly white Protestant Christian society.

The aim of this brief article is to highlight in the baldest terms possible some of the ways in which groups of non-white minorities have sought to maintain their religious practices in an alien, or at least *new*, territory. It is first necessary, however, to point to one or two aspects of the general situation in which non-white ethnic minorities find themselves in Britain.

Migration, state and religion

In formal terms Britain is a Christian Protestant society. In reality, however, Protestantism has given way to secularism which is based on a rationalism common to most of North West Europe. This subsequent dual character of British society—Christian but secular—is not only reflected in the dominant

* The authors are based in the Centre for Research in Ethnic Relations at the University of Warwick.

ideologies informing social action; it is also evident in the composition of a number of major institutions of the country. In a strict constitutional sense church and state are not separated in England. In practice, however, state and church are neither rigidly separated nor too tightly compacted. At the same time, they are inextricably bound together as a result of a peculiar island-history which marks Britain off from continental experience. More specifically, the Queen of England (and indeed also of Scotland, Wales, North Ireland and a large number of Commonwealth countries, particularly those which have not declared themselves republics) is both the constitutional head of state and formal head of the Established or Anglican (state) Church. The monarch does not, of course, exercise the *real* authority enshrined in these offices: the Prime Minister and the Archbishop of Canterbury, respecively, are the *effective* heads of these offices.

This separation of the *formal* and the *actual* manifests itself in nearly all aspects of British life. For example, the 1944 and 1988 Education Acts stipulate the compulsory teaching of religion in schools, the school day commencing with a collective act of worship. In a court of law it is customary to take the oath on the Bible. Both Parliament and city council meetings begin with a prayer, irrespective of the political party in office. Few people have any strong objections to this because the British political tradition is not characterized by the kind of anti-clericalism common, for example, in France. One reason for this difference is that the contention between church and state in England was entered upon and resolved long before it was broached in France. In the established church clergymen officiate at marriages and these are automatically valid before the law. An ancient law of blasphemy protects the teachings of the established (official) Church of England. This law has not generally been invoked in recent times but it can be acted upon, as in 1977 when anti-pornography campaigner, Mary Whitehouse, successfully secured prosecution of *Gay News* for publishing a poem concerning a centurion and the lifting of Christ's body from the cross.

Long established minorities such as the Catholics (mostly Irish immigrants but also including prominent aristocratic families) and the Jews have, from the last century, enjoyed freedom of worship along with other civil rights. For example, many Catholic and Jewish schools have enjoyed the status of being grant-aided (partly financed by the state) independent establishments. Marriages may be officiated by Catholic priests and rabbis, which are valid before the law. Clergymen from other churches may also obtain a certificate enabling them to have the same prerogatives, but only clergymen of the official church receive these certificates automatically. Whilst priests of other religions such as Sikhism, Hinduism and Islam may officiate at weddings, it is necessary for an official from the civil marriage registry to be present.

Short of man-power for a burgeoning post-war economy, Britain in the years 1948–1962 encouraged the migration of labour from her ex-colonies and decolonizing territories in South East Asia, the Indian subcontinent (now Pakistan, India, Bangladesh, and Sri Lanka) and the English-speaking Caribbean. The new workers were to fill the gaps created by the upward mobility of the native workforce in the wake of the economic revival which Europe as a whole enjoyed in the immediate post-war years. During the first phase of this process, which was to significantly change the *cityscape* of Britain, such migrants were (as Table 1 shows) mainly men; especially with respect to people from the Indian subcontinent. With the threat after the mid-1950s to stop immigration from the *non-white* parts of the British imperial enclosure into Britain, many of these workers decided to send for their wives and children so that, should they decide to stay for longer than originally intended, they would at least be able to exist as a (nuclear) family unit. Thus, from the late 1950s the pattern of migration to Britain changed as Table 2 illustrates. Young working men were joined by their families, and with the entry of *families* communities soon developed. Subsequently, the intention of returning home with some cash in pocket to extend the family holding, etc., subsided, and the more protracted struggle to establish homes in Britain commenced. These new homes and new communities were to be established mainly in the decaying inner-cities (central areas of major cities), which were soon deserted by the middle and investing classes.

Table 1
Population by country of birth, age and sex, Great Britain 1981.

	Age (Percentages)						
Country of birth	Under 16	16–29	30–44	45–59 (women) 45–64 (men)	60 and over (women)65 and over (men)	All persons (thousands = 100%)	Males per 100 females
New Commonwealth and Pakistan	9	33	29	22	6	1472	107

Source: Labour Force Survey, OPCS, 1981 (22.2.83).

The process of entry and settlement of Britain's non-white population in the post-war years were, therefore, largely unsupervised, unplanned, and developed without much direct state assistance. The exceptions to this were the entry of Asians from Kenya in 1966, Uganda in 1972/3 and Malawi in 1976. These moments were punctuated by political dramas as the British government of the day attempted to gain maximum political kudos from these crises by the simple and expected act of honouring their international, legal, commitments.

One of several notable factors which tends to distinguish the experience of entry and settlement of the non-white population in Britain from similar experiences on the Continent, is the fact that in Britain people from the former empire had formal rights of citizenship. Within the former empire, individuals enjoyed a differential sets of rights as British subjects with allegiance to His or Her Majesty, the King or Queen of England (Goulbourne, in press). With the end of empire and the mushrooming of new nation-states around the globe there emerged out of the former empire the international, voluntary, association known as the

Table 2

Persons resident in private households with head of household born in the New Commonwealth and Pakistan (NCWP), by country of origin.

(figures in brackets = Great Britain %)

	Caribbean	India	Pakistan	Bangladesh	East Africa	Far East	Mediterranean	Remainder	Total NCWP
All persons born:									
inside UK	372,558	261,206	118.252	16,939	48,673	39,742	79,315	57,907	895,592
outside UK	272,186	412,498	177,209	47,622	132,648	80,381	90,763	98,346	1,311,653
Total persons	545,744	673,704	295,461	64,561	181,321	120,123	170,078	156,253	2,207,245
	(24.7)	(30.5)	(13.4)	(2.9)	(8.2)	(5.4)	(7.7)	(7.2)	(100)

Source: OPCS, Census 1981 op. cit.

Commonwealth.[1] Migration from these countries in the Caribbean came to a virtual end by the mid-1960s, as a result of the 1962 Commonwealth Immigration Act and of Caribbean migration to the more prosperous and seemingly less hostile North American continent. With respect, however, to the Indian subcontinent and particularly East and Central Africa, 'Asians' continued, as we have noted, to come to Britain. Not surprisingly, Britain has tried to shun her responsibilities for some of her subjects abroad: in 1968, 1971 and 1981/3 immigration and nationality laws were passed restricting entry of non-white people into Britain even though they held British passports. Traditionally, children born in Britain had, automatically, British citizenship under the *jus soli* principle (that is to say that the *place* of birth, not the nationality of the parents, determines a person's nationality). The 1981 Nationality Act changed this practice which had been a cardinal principle of British nationality law since the Middle Ages and had been reaffirmed in the comprehensive and consolidating 1948 Nationality Act which remained on the staute books until 1981/3. Since 1983, when the new Act took effect, the parents of a child born on British soil must also have been British citizens for the child to enjoy the status of British citizen.

All individuals, however—who are neither members of the House of Lords and are deemed to be sane—coming to Britain from the Commonwealth may vote after a year's residence, become members of the armed forces, the civil service and serve on juries; they may also stand for local and national elected offices. (This situation also obtains in some other Commonwealth countries. And this is especially so with respect to Caribbean Commonwealth countries, particularly where the right to

[1] People from Pakistan constituted a special case, because in 1971, as a result of Britain and the Commonwealth's recognition of the newly formed state of Bangladesh (formerly East Pakistan), Pakistan left the Club. The new PPP government under Benazir Bhutto is presently (mid-October, 1989) seeking re-entry into the Club at its annual heads of government meeting in Malaysia. This is most likely to be welcomed by all members. From 1971 to the present individuals from Pakistan living in Britain have been treated as if they are from a Commonwealth country.

vote and other rights of citizenship are concerned.) Since the 1987 general elections and subsequent local government elections, there are now over 250 non-white elected local councillors throughout England and Wales and four elected members of the House of Commons (Diane Abbot, Paul Boateng, Bernie Grant, and Keith Vaz —*see*, Goulbourne, 1990). Lord Chitnis and Lord Pitt have long been members of the hereditary and nominated upper House of Lords. In some wards (in local authorities) Asian and Afro-Caribbean groups form the majority and in at least one parliamentary constituency they came close to forming a majority of voters. This does not mean, however, that voters in these areas will necessarily return candidates from their specific communities, because like other voters in Britain, party loyalty is the first consideration.

For some very sound historical, sociological, and ideological reasons which cannot be gone into here, most non-white Britishers have tended to vote for the Labour Party. The Conservative and Social & Liberal Democratic parties have also attracted a number of Afro-Caribbean and Asian politicians. Britain's Afro-Caribbean and Asian populations have, however, expressed much of their political concerns through non-party and non-parliamentary vehicles. Street protests and riots (in 1980, 1981, and 1985) over police brutality or right-wing vandalism, campaigns against deportation, poor education, housing, etc., have until recently been much more prominent or salient than participation in the established political parties. In some areas such protest have led to the setting-up of commissions and/or committees of inquiry to conduct detailed and independent investigations. For example, the Scarman Inquiry followed the 1981 Brixton Riots and in 1981 and 1985 two reports on education— Rampton and Swan, respectively—were published. The issues some groups have raised about life in Britain have long been seen to be more important and urgent than most of the issues raised about events in their original homeland. This is not to say, however, that homeland politics have not continued to be of great importance to some groups, as we shall see below.

A number of legal measures have been enacted to control the

more rapacious aspects of racism against non-white peoples. These measures were enacted as a result of protest against racial discrimination by minorities themselves, with support from liberal and progressive individuals and groups in society, as well as the will of elements of the state to maintain social peace and cohesion. In a paper of this kind some of these measures can only be mentioned in passing. They include the 1966 Local Government Act (Section 11) which makes special provisions for local authorities to try to correct or control the massive imbalance between people from the New Commonwealth and the native white population. Another legal measure is the Urban Programme. Established in the late 1960s in response to the growing concern over urban and social deprivation. This measure was reformed and expanded in 1977 following the publication of a discussion (White Paper) document entitled *Policy for the Inner Cities*. Although this measure does not specifically mention ethnic minorities, some of the geographical areas affected are predominantly occupied by non-white ethnic minorities. This programme is administered and financed by both the central and local governments. A third example is the 1976 Race Relations Act. This established a Commission for Racial Equality (CRE) with a broader brief than its 1968 predecessor, the Race Relations Board. The CRE is empowered to conduct investigations into incidents of racial discrimination; it may also point to indirect discrimination and make recommendations to the Home Office (interior department) for legal changes it considers necessary for 'good race relations' in the country. The legislation also called upon local authorities—the bodies primarily responsible for the delivery of educational, health, social security, etc., services to citizens—to take steps to ensure equality of opportunity and good race relations (Section 71); as a result they have adopted equal opportunities policies and set up equal opportunity and race relations units. The enthusiasm with which many radical and progressive local authorities tackled the problem was soon undermined, however, by a widespread and concerted attack on local government by the Conservative government from the mid-1980s. The decline of local democracy is likely to narrow and restrict the space in which minorities have been able to articulate their demands because the traditional decentralization of government in Britain meant that local authorities provided the most appropriate forums for citizens, including monorities, to raise specific grievances. Decentralization, however, coupled with the relative separation of functional sources of authority, has tended to encourage the strategy of trying to formulate specific policies for specific groups, at both national and local levels of politics and society in Britain.

These general points provide a background—albeit incomplete—against which several more specific points may be made about the religious dimension of non-white minorities in contemporary Britain.

Religion and non-white minorities

Ethnic minorities from Asia and the Caribbean have greatly enriched the religious dimension of British life in the decades since entry and settlement from the 1940s. From the Indian subcontinent has come, Islam, Sikhism, Buddhism, and a variety of Hindu sects. These religions are distinctly different from the mainstream Christian traditions out of which secular society has emerged during the last several centuries and do not, therefore, settle too easily with the secular norms which inform social and political action. With respect to people from the Caribbean, all religious expressions—even the most radical, namely, Rastafarianism—are derived from broad Christian traditions. This does not mean, however, that the forms of practice they have developed are the same as those usually practised in Britain. Indeed, if the much talked about pluralism of British society means anything at all, it must surely mean that the religious contours of society have become immensely more complex and pluralistic than perhaps at any other time in the country's history. Several general observations may be made concerning this increasing religious pluralism in Britain.

In the first place, all religious groups have become, in one way or another, *minority* groups in Britain. This may be partly explained by the secular nature of contemporary British society. Essentially, secularism has been marked by the decline in church attendance by the vast majority of people in Britain. In most churches on a typical Sunday, the majority of worshippers tend to be the elderly and the very young. As members of the latter group mature, there is a tendency for their attendance to fall off. Events such as marriage, the christening or baptism of a child, or death in the family usually occasion the presence in church of those in the prime of life. Otherwise, only the most devout Christians are to be seen inside church on an ordinary Sunday.

This low turn-out has been particularly true for the established, official Chuch of England (or Anglicans), but in general terms it is also the case for some of the other main Christian denominations such as the Methodists, the Salvation Army, and the Baptists. On the other hand, the Adventists and a long list of popular Evangelical denominations which are usually described as Pentecostal churches, are generally believed to have thriving numbers of devout members. Whilst, therefore, in some quarters religion—measured in terms of attendance at the site of worship—may be declining in the lives of the vast majority of people deemed to be Christians, this is not evenly the case. In general terms, however, church leaders are genuinely concerned about the extent to which people take religion seriously. It may therefore be suggested that increasing secularism has led to the vast majority of people refraining from practising any particular religion and thereby rendering all religious persuasions into minority communities. This includes the official church: indeed, it is generally said that there are more practising Muslims in Britain than there are active members of the Church of England.

This leads to a second general observation about the religious situation in Britain. At the same time as the official church is declining in terms of regular attendance and perhaps influence, non-Christian religions have become attractive to some members of the majority white society as well as members of the non-white ethnic minorities who may have a Christian background. These non-Christian religions include the Bahai faith, Buddhism, Islam, the Hari Krishna movement, and so forth. These would appear to meet the religious needs of some who may be dissatisfied with the more materialist-oriented norms of contemporary society with which Western Christianity now seems to be too much at home. Sometimes, of course, the attraction would appear to be nothing more than a fascination with the apparently exotic and the strange. Other times conversion seems to be genuine. It is not surprising, therefore, that some of the most staunch defenders of Islam in the furore which ensued over Salman Rushdie's *Satanic Verses* in 1988/9 have been converts such as the former pop-star Cat Stevens.

With the notable exception of Northern Ireland, however, religious difference in Britain is not, *per se*, a major divisive factor although it is sometimes marshalled in support of arguments which suggest that broad cultural differences will divide a supposedly homogeneous Britain.

A third observation may be made about the general religious situation in Britain today. Like elsewhere, religion is becoming a rallying point for those who, for one reason or another, feel alienated, excluded, or threatened. Subsequently, the great compromise effected between religion and the secular state in Britain is being called into question. When, recently, the effective and spiritual head of the Church of England, the Archbishop of Canterbury (Dr. Robert Runcie) criticized the visible increase in greed and the decline of Christian charity in Britain, this was taken to be a severe criticism of the Conservative government led by Margaret Thatcher. More significantly, however, has been the impact of Muslim militancy against what they see as the encroachment of secular values upon their faith. Whilst this has been expressing itself in a variety of demands, as discussed below, by far the most spectacular militant outburst which brings into sharp focus the religious and the secular, has been the Rushdie affair. This general point may, however, be illustrated by reference to both Sikhism and Islam.

Sikhs and Khalistan

Britain is estimated to have the single largest population of Sikhs living outside India. Estimates of their numbers vary wildly and as many as 400,000 has been mentioned. Of course, it is not possible to give a safe figure for any ethnic minority in Britain because enumeration on a nation-wide basis has not, up to now, taken sufficient account of ethnic origins; enumerators have been much more concerned with *place* of birth, as Tables 1 and 2 illustrate. Regional population studies, however, sometimes include religious affiliation where this is a crucial factor in determining ethnicity. For example, the city of Leicester—the site of major settlement by Asians, particularly from East Africa—accounted for its Asian residents in terms of religious and linguistic groupings thus: Gujerati-speaking Hindus 36,100, Punjabi-speaking Sikhs 9600, Gujerati-speaking Muslims 2900, Urdu-speaking Muslims 1200 (Leicester City council, 1984). The important points to note here are that the Sikh population is a relatively large and is a highly visible one amongst the ethnic minorities of Britain, and that events in India, particularly since the mid-1980s, have greatly influenced their political behaviour. And it is crucial to note that for devout Sikhs there can be no sensible distinction between religious and political beliefs.

Since the early 1970s, a handful of radical Sikhs has called for an independent state of Khalistan to be carved out of Punjab in North India. But until the storming of their Golden Temple in the city of Amritsar on 5 June, 1984 by the Indian army, the demand did not attract the support of devout Sikhs anywhere. With this dramatic event Sikhs everywhere felt that their religion was seriously threatened and overnight the militancy, for which they are traditionally renowned, was rekindled. This has been noticeably so in Britain, especially between 1984 and 1986/7. Not only is there a sizeable Sikh presence here but, perhaps more importantly, there was a special relationship between the Sikhs and the British during the colonial days; and there are still echoes of this today in the collective consciousness of both the Sikhs and those in Britain who were, or are, familiar with India.

The Sikhs first came under the British Raj through a series of treaties, typically following colonial wars of conquest. In the Indian Mutiny of 1857 the Sikhs supported the British and, in turn, the British recruited some of their most loyal soldiers from amongst the martial Sikhs. They were also highly favoured with respect to the land redistribution which occurred as part of the land reform scheme pursued by the imperial power in the highly fertile and well irrigated Punjab. In short, the interest that British Sikhs have shown in developments in their historic homeland is not insignificant, nor is it surprising.

Events in India, particularly since the mid-1980s, have served to highlight the presence of Sikhs in Britain. In the past, perhaps more than any other group, the Sikhs were the most noticeable of colonial peoples who settled in Britain. This was largely due to their distinctive physical appearance which—following the teachings of the Tenth and last *Guru*, the soldier-saint Gobind Singh—is an hallmark of their religion. They were, therefore, from early on in their sojourn and settlement concerned about gaining rights which would enable them to maintain their own distinctive religious-communal life in their new home: these included the right for baptised Sikhs to wear turbans (Bidwell, 1987) instead of motor-cycle helmets or bus conductors' or school caps, and to carry the *kirpan* (a long knife). Typically, following the struggle for recognition, British society has responded favourably to these demands, and Sikhs frequently express their satisfaction with the adjustments made to their faith in certain areas of public life. Interviewed, the typical secretary of a typical *gurdwara*[1] will stress the fact that Sikhs have done well for themselves in Britain, and that, unlike India, Britain has left them alone to worship in their own manner.

Not surprisingly, however, it is the *Keshadhari* and not the

[1] The *gurdwara* is a place of worship but it is also a central meeting place for the devout. But the *gurdwara* is also more than this. A crucial part of its surrounds is the *langar* (kitchen) where food is always available for any visitor. It is therefore something of a refuge for the hungry. In a non-Sikh community this institution is obviously of vital importance as a meeting point where Sikhs can freely share their daily cares, concerns, and so on.

Sahajdhari[1] Sikhs who have attracted attention and, in the colonial period, gained the firm support of the British in India.
This fact has prompted some observers to remark that the development of Sikhism from the middle of the last century to the
middle of the present one, was largely due to the British presence
in the subcontinent (*see*, for example, Nayer & Singh, 1984).
One implication here is that, left alone, the reformist Sikh movement, which borrowed from the two major religions present in
India at the time—Islam and Hinduism—might have melted
into one or the other of these world faiths after a radical birth
in the sixteenth century. In India today Sikhs feel acutely threatened by Hindus and those Sikhs who have migrated to Britain
(or were born in Britain) are deeply aware of a need to make the
Sikh cause in the 'homeland' clear to the rest of the world.

Not surprisingly, as in all such movements, there are several
competing politico-religious groups in Britain vying for pre-
eminence in the campaign to organize their cause. One body,
however, which, for much of the 1980s was able to claim the
support of most groups has been the Khalistan[2] Council founded
by Dr. Jagjit Singh Chohan (a medical doctor and former minister in the state government of Punjab) who was also the first
politician to call for a separate state of Khalistan in 1971 (*see*,
Goulbourne, in press). In turn, the Council has sought to be
affiliated to the Panthic Committee based in the *Akal Takht* (the
body concerned with temporal/political matters) in Amritsar. In
1987, for example, the Council's president was able at its third
annual convention in Slough, London, to state that he had the
support of the following diverse groups—Babbar Khalsa International, the World Sikh Organization, Akhand Kirtani Jatha of

----

[1] *Keshadharis* adhere to the famous Five Ks of the Sikhs: *kesh* (the uncut
hair, like the Nazarites in ancient Judaism); the *kangha* (a comb); the *kirpan*
(a sword/long knife); *kachha* (a pair of shorts) and *kara* (a steel bangle).
Sahajdhari Sikhs are those who refer to themselves as the 'slow adopters'
because they do not adhere to the Five Ks instituted by the Tenth Guru
Gobind Singh.
[2] *Khalistan* denotes the state of the 'community of the pure' or the
'brother/sisterhood' of devout, baptised Sikhs; it is derived from the *khalsa*
which was instituted by the warrior-priest Tenth Guru Gobind Singh.

the United Kingdom, the Sikh Youth Movement, the Dal Khalsa International, and the International Sikh Youth Federation. This proliferation of groups, all seeking to espouse the cause of the Sikh faith and homeland in North India, reflects the democratic spirit of Sikhism which also imbues the movement for a free and independent state of Khalistan.

The great misunderstanding, from which Sikhs in Britain suffers, revolves around the *religious* mode of articulation which clouds much of the harsh economic and political grievances they have against the central government of India. In a largely secular society, the emphasis placed on the religious foundation, of what could be defended as a political cause, is bound to lead to much misunderstanding. Subsequently, in general terms, the Khalistani cause is not perceived as one which deserves the support of progressive political groups in Britain. Indeed, there has been a tendency for the Sikh cause to be defended in parliament by politicians on the Right of British politics. On the other hand, the impact of the demand for an independent Sikh state of Khalistan may steadily remove from public view the more fundamental religious concerns of the devout Sikh in Britain and the more political aspect of Sikhism gain undue prominence. Sikhs, however, see politics and religion to be inextricably bound together and in discussions over these matters leaders frequently point to the relationship between the Church of England, the Queen, and the British state as an example of this relationship. They see no good reason, therefore, why they should not seek to express religion and political demands together.

The Muslims

As with other groups, it is difficult to obtain precise figures on the numbers of Muslims in Britain because the national census does not include a question on religion. However, it is possible to formulate an estimate of the Muslim population on the basis of data on country of birth or country of origin. The latest census (1981) identifies 398,624 residents born in countries where Islam is the main religion, that is 0.07% of the total population. People from the Indian subcontinent constitute the main group of Muslims in Britain. To the 295,461 people of Pakistani origin and 64,561 of Bangladeshi origin (both figures includes those born in Britain) must be added Muslims from India and Muslim Asians from East Africa (Commission for Racial Equality, 1985).

Community life is structured by family networks and by the mosques. This structuring results from the characteristic of Islam as a *din*, governing not only religious practice and morality but social relationships, marriage, divorce, family relations, economics, politics, and the most humble actions of everyday life. Muslim leaders have expressed their concern for the development of Islam in Britain and the moral well-being of its followers, particularly where the second generation is concerned. They portray Western society as meaningless, rootless, characterized by crime, juvenile delinquency, riots, the collapse of marriages, and sexual promiscuity. They postulate that Islam can provide an alternative lifestyle in Britain: Islam is presented as an ideological movement confronted with the ideology of the West and a materialist secular society. Muslim leaders also take pride in saying that Islam forms good citizens.

Mosques are numerous and varied and new mosques are created every year: there are some 500 mosques throughout Britain and in Birmingham, the second largest city in Britain and where there is a large Muslim population, there are about 50 mosques. There may be several mosques in the same area and sometimes more than one in the same street. This can be explained by two main factors: the existence of diverse branches of Islam and the national and regional bases of the mosques, each group founding its own. The varieties of Islam to be found in Britain are those practised and founded in the Indian peninsula. Only a small minority of people are Shia while the vast majority are Sunni Hanafi. There is a vast Sufi community (mostly Barelwis) and the UK Islamic Mission, the British branch of Jamaati Islami, which is a reformist movement, has gained prominence through its campaign against Rushdie's *Satanic Verses*

Mosques fulfil several functions and constitute a pole of community activities. They are first and foremost places of worship but also a social hub around which families gather for the Muslim holy celebrations. They generally possess a *medersa*, a koranic school, attended by dozens sometimes hundreds of children (depending on the size of the mosque). The larger mosques teach the language of origin and may have a variety of services comprising library, bookshop, and funeral provisions, an advice centre and community facilities for the elderly, the youth, or women. Mosques also play the role of pressure groups and act as intermediaries between Muslims and the wider society.

Muslims, like other non-white ethnic minorities, vote mainly for the Labour Party and candidates who are Muslim by religion and culture have been elected onto city councils. In Birmingham, for instance, there are 8 councillors of Muslim origin out of 15 ethnic councillors with Asian and Caribbean backgrounds (there are 117 councillors in Birmingham). The mosques and other Muslim leaders and spokespersons have put forward a number of demands regarding their faith and have negotiated with the municipality over these and related issues.

One important question is that of education because Muslims wish to safeguard Islam among their young who are heavily influenced by their school experience. The decentralization of authority and the less than secular character of schooling in Britain has made it possible for Muslims to obtain some favourable results for the schooling of their children. There is general agreement among many Muslim parents and mosque leaders that the school curriculum should incorporate the teaching of Islam. A number of demands concerning the morning assembly, religious education, holidays for the main Muslim celebrations, such as *Eid ul Fitr* and *Eid ul Adha* and prayer facilities in the school (especially for the Friday congregational prayer), have been expressed. A whole series of issues arise alongside these demands: the availability of halal food (the animal being slaughtered according to Muslim rite), exemption from sex education and respect for modesty where girls are concerned (including a demand for non-mixed physical education and swimming classes) modest clothing (the uniform is unacceptable as skirts are compulsory) and a possible exemption from dancing, music, and drama classes. Some councils have been able to satisfy some of the demands from Muslim organizations on some of these questions. Some, however, such as those concerning single-sex education and grant-aided Muslim schools have proved to be more intractable. As noted earlier, more recently, several Muslim organizations and mosques have been campaigning nationally for the banning of the *Satanic Verses* and the extension of the blasphemy law to cover Islam.

Religion and Caribbean communities

West Indians are a culturally and politically highly secular people. The moral and ethical values which inform their social and political practices and oraganizational structures are, however, deeply rooted within a broad Christian tradition. This is true not only for those who are active, practising Christians, but also for those who would claim to have no religion at all, or who, alternatively, would express a preference for Rastafarianism or Islam. This is, of course, a paradox. which finds its explanation in a complex and continuous historical drama which has been enacted in the Caribbean over the last three centuries or so. The result has been the development of a culture which is very proximate to the majority (native) culture of Britain but also exhibits distinctive features some of which have their sources in the African past.

But this very proximity has meant that Caribbean people in Britain—mainly of African descent but by no means exclusively so—confront a complex situation of exclusion by the majority society. One of the first responses to this unexpected experience of exclusion was the emergence of what is being called the black-led churches. Perhaps because practising Christians from the Caribbean felt most deeply the hurt which comes from the experience of exclusion from the gatherings of the devout, they were also amongst the first West Indians to begin to organize so as to meet their specific needs. There were, of course, other factors which encouraged the founding and growth of black-led churches. It has been suggested, for example, that the strong evangelicism of West Indian Christians and their more express-ive form of worship marked them off from their white British brethren and sisters. In any event, there has developed a dynamic practising Christian community among West Indians through-out Britain. These churches are believed to be rather bouyant: in 1979 one observer estimated that these denominations were experiencing a growth of 5% (Charman, 1979, p. 44) whilst a later commentator (Howard, 1987, p. 11) gave a slightly higher estimate of growth.

One result of this has been to unify many Christians who belong hitherto to different denominations. Individuals who were brought up in the Caribbean as Anglicans or Methodists, for example, often joined one of the various churches generally called Pentecostals in Britain. There are still many practising Christians from the Caribbean who have continued to worship in their original denominations (Anglican, Methodist, Baptist, Congregational, etc.) and increasingly many have come to see it as their duty to insist on changes in these churches. In general, they raise the problems of racism and the need to have greater black representation in church leadership. In the Church of England, for example, there is only one black bishop (Wilfred Wood of Croydon) and at the last meeting of general synod (the Church's parliament) the proposal to have a number of seats reserved for black members was heatedly debated.

There is a variety of churches which are generally called Pente-costals. These include the Elim, Assembly of God, Church of God, New Testament, etc., denominations which all, to one degree or another, stress the importance of speaking in tongues (as on the Day of Pentecost, hence the name), baptism by full immersion, literal interpretation of the Bible, and so forth. These churches are not exclusively black or Caribbean. They relate easily with other churches of the same denomination throughout the United Kingdom and have close relations with American, Caribbean, African, etc., churches. In the United Kingdom, membership of the black-led churches are mainly black but there are also white members. Perhaps what is most distinctive about them is the fact that they are founded and led by individuals from the Caribbean or of Caribbean background. The manner of worship is more lively and musically accessible. They tend to be highly democratic but in the past leadership depended almost entirely on the individual pastor's charisma. With the establishment of training colleges (for example, the New Testament Church of God training college in Northampton), the ownership of premises and a more stable membership, many of these churches have strengthened themselves as permanent features in particular communities throughout the country. They have also long served as one of the main institutions to have kept alive aspects of Caribbean culture (for example, music) in Britain. These churches do not require to be treated any differently from other Christian denominations.[1]

The only religious group from the Caribbean whose practices are such that its devotees would welcome a change in the law of the land are the Rastafarians. This springs from their belief that marijuana (ganga) is a gift of God to be enjoyed; to smoke this weed is, of course, to break the law. This principle of Rastafarianism perhaps all too frequently leaves the impression that the sect is disrespectful of the law. Their religion is, however, a peaceful one which stresses the equality of all people, justice for all, and love. Started in Jamaica in the 1930s, Rastafarianism spread throughout Britain's inner city areas in the 1970s. Mass black youth unemployment, police harassment on the streets, disillusionment with British institutions, and so forth, provided the necessary social conditions in which Rastafarianism could flourish. Additionally, its stress on the need for black people outside Africa to return there, its interpretation of the Old Testament as prophesying the coming of Haile Selassie (of Ethiopia) and Jah (God), its description of the places black people away from Africa live as Babylon (after the ancient Israelites' experience in Babylonia), seemed to provide some meaning to the lives of disenchanted British black youths as the recession deepened in the 1970s.

[1] Although the Seventh Day Adventists have established the very successful John Laughborough school in London it is not exclusively black.

Both in Britain and Jamaica Rastafarians created and developed the popular reggae music, with the late super-star Bob Marley being one of its most well-known proponents. The Rastas (named after Ras Tafari, Haile Selassie, crowned Emperor of Ethiopia in 1930, who was overthrown in the Revolution in 1973 and died soon after) preach the virtue of a simple life, clean living, a vegetarian diet and the wearing of the hair uncut and knotted to form *dreadlocks*. In the early 1970s a number of Rasta organizations from Jamaica, such as The Twelve Tribes of Israel, established themselves in England and Rasta *reasoning* (a ritualistic but open form of discussion through which doctrines are explained) became common. Perhaps because of its stress on equality or perhaps because it is a sect still in its infancy (as compared to other religions) Rastafarianism does not have established hierarchical leadership structures. Apart from its creative music and art, Rastafarianism has provided a major critique of the mental and spiritual domination of black people in the African diaspora. This critique, which includes a call to redemption in a return from exile, is expressed in the language of the King James' Version of the Bible, particularly the Old Testament. But the basic message is much the same as is found in Franz Fanon's *Black Skin White Mask*, and has been echoed in many nationalist critiques of colonialism.

Conclusion

These general comments about Britain's relatively new minorities from the Indian subcontinent and the Caribbean in no way exhausts the rich religious culture which is still emerging. The ways of life that some of these religions bring to Britain pose definite challenges for some of what has long been taken for granted in a secular society. In other cases the culture and institutions of the majority indigenous population are enriched and made more varied. Perhaps expectedly but sadly, neither the challenges these religions pose nor the contributions they are capable of making are likely to be smoothly interwoven into the national fabric.

Select Bibliography

Bidwell, Sydney 1987. *The Turban Victory*. The Sikh Missionary Society, Southall.

Cashmore, E. E. 1984. *The Rastafarians*. Report No. 64. Minority Rights Group, London.

Charman, P. 1979. *Reflections: Black and White Christians in the City*. Zebra Project.

Commission for Racial Equality. 1985. *Ethnic Minorities in Britain, Statistical information on the pattern of settlement*. CRE, London.

Goulbourne, H. (ed.) 1990. *Some Aspects of Black Politics in Britain*. Avebury-Gower, Aldershot.

Goulbourne, H. (in press). *The Communal Option: Nationalism and Ethnicity in Post-Imperial Britain*.

Howard, V. 1987. *A Report on Afro-Caribbean Christianity in Britain*. Department of Theology & Religious Studies, University of Leeds.

Joly, Danièle, 1987. *Making a place for Islam in British Society: Muslims in Birmingham*. Research Papers No. 4. Centre for Research in Ethnic Relations, Coventry.

Labour Force Survey. Office of Population Censuses and Surveys (OPCS), 1981 (22 February, 1983).

Leicester City Council, 1984. *Survey of Leicester, 1983: Initial Report of Survey*. Leicester City Council.

Nagar, K. & Singh, Kushwant, 1984. *Tragedy of Punjab: Operation Bluestar and After*. Vision Books, New Delhi.

Rex, John, 1988. *The Ghetto and the Underclass. Essays on Race and Social Policy*. Avebury-Gower, Aldershot.

Rex, John & Moore, R. 1967. *Race, Community and Conflict*. Oxford University Press, Oxford.

Shackle, C. 1984. *The Sikhs*. Report No. 65. Minority Rights Group, London.

A Perspective on the Post-Sacred World: Christianity and Islam

*Gianni Baget Bozzo**

In a number of countries at present, we are witnessing a return to religion in its various forms. The most common manifestation of this tendency is the declared belief that religious discourse is meaningful. This return to religion is perhaps due to the diminished influence of atheistic Utopianism or of the notion that the world has no transcendent dimension. The human adventure has reached such a point that the concept of nature itself is outdated, just as is the certainty that there exists some immutable realm of reality. Nature was synonymous with God in the agnostic and atheistic language of the 19th century and the first half of the 20th. No longer do we believe that history or nature are informed by some inherent rationality, that they are both explicable in terms of human reason. The transparent association between reason, nature, and history lies at the source of all the political ideologies that have been propounded over the past two centuries. Nowadays, human endeavour and technological advances have taken us beyond the limits of the concept of nature by which human activity was seen to be bounded and within which its possibilities were defined. Materialism retains the same attributes of a divine Creator that are to be found in the Judaeo-Christian religion. We seek to return ever to the origin of things: evolution implies beginning, and for this reason

* Gianni Baget Bozzo is a Catholic priest and a journalist. He is the author of several works on the history of Christian democracy and Italian politics, as well as numerous writings on theology and the philosophy of religion.

the *future can* and indeed *must be interpreted as an extension of the past*. Just like traditional religion, materialism seeks to reassure human beings against the uncertainty of the future and the deficiency of the *senses*. Reason itself is but sense, and the future is already contained within its causes. There is nothing new, except in the extent to which reason, nature, and history become thoroughly interwoven and attain to the full development that is already prefigured in their origins.

The weakening of materialism is due, curiously, to developments in science and technology which have shown how man, by meddling with the atom, the cell, or the gene, can modify the very conditions of nature, produce forces which nature has not placed at man's disposal, and act upon the qualities of human life at its very source by modifying our genetic heritage. Man has the capacity to destroy, without knowing it, the very possibility of life within the earth's ecosystem, just as he can now go beyond the frontiers of the planet. Man has shown himself to be something more than what used to be understood by 'natural'. It is this very success of science and technology that has undermined scientism and materialism as viable systems of thought. Since the latter had presented themselves as alternatives to the concept of God while continuing to fulfil the same role, religious language found itself released from the realms of the unreal and the nonsensical to which rationalism and materialism had consigned it.

All of this has given rise to religious phenomena that are characterized by the quest for an individual and collective experience of the divine. It is not, however, upon this aspect of the question—upon the re-emergence of the mystical as a means of understanding and expressing the world—that we wish to focus our attention, but upon one of the consequences of this resurgence of religious language as a meaningful medium: that is, specifically upon its political uses.

The political use of religion

It is strange that this question should come to the fore after an event, Vatican Council II, which marked the height of the Church's endeavour to come to terms with the 'modern' world, that is, with the world as it has emerged from the phases of rationalism and materialism. One of the consequences of the latter was the collapse of the concept of the Christian state and even of the Christian political party, the severing of any systematic connection between religion and politics, as expressed in traditional terms such as 'Christendom' and in the notion that whole populations equally professed Christianity within a civic context. In its various forms, in fact, the relationship between Church and society has now become the most pressing issue for the Catholic Church and the Protestant Churches alike.

It is no less strange that politico-religious discourse should have discovered in the mass media, and above all in television, the best means of making an impact upon society at large. Television gives an impression of immediacy to the message that is communicated, because of the appearance of the human face upon the screen. It serves more than any other medium to distinguish the sacred from the religious. The sacred, by its very nature, demands to be seen in isolation, to be distinguished from all that is profane. It requires its own space and time, just as it requires men who express through their lives this same separation of the sacred from the profane. In the Catholic world, one may cite as an example of this the image of the Pope such as he was perceived before John-Paul II. The Pope discharged his office from the Vatican or, at the furthest, from Castel Gandolfo. His sacred status within the world was defined by the very fact that he reigned over a sovereign State, however tiny. Rome was the centre of pilgrimage: Catholics went to visit the Pope, not vice versa.

With John-Paul II, this sacred status has been altogether abandoned. The Pope now aims to exploit the means of direct communication offered by the media; in this way, he has become an integral part of the political theatre as public spectacle.

Mediation and isolation are no longer meaningful concepts in the case of a Pope who entrusts his message more to gesture and presence than to the spoken word. The message itself is one of reassurance. The first words which he spoke to the world, in the encyclical *Redemptor Hominis*, were 'Do not be afraid'. This theme of security was taken up again, in more dramatic form, in his last encyclical, the *Rei Socialis Sollicitudo*, in which the Pope declared, with all the authority of his office, that man's earthly adventure would be brought to a happy conclusion. The Pope wishes that the Church discharge its role in today's society precisely as a *reassuring presence*. And his appearance throughout the world, amplified as it is by television, reinforces the *immediacy of his presence*, that is, the very antithesis of the isolation and mediation that once constituted the role of the sacred as opposed to the profane. If the Pope does not want priests, as individuals, to engage in political activities, it is because he wants the Church as a whole to bring a reassuring presence to bear in human affairs. One certainly cannot deny the immediacy of the Church's presence in Poland or the Philippines. Such places provide examples of the Church playing an active role in the social and political life of the community. Cardinal Glemp and Cardinal Sin alike have actively intervened in political affairs, determining thereby the destiny of the State and its citizens. For the last examples of Church intervention on this scale one has to go back to medieval times. Throughout the Protestant Reformation and the Catholic counter-Reformation, it was the monarch who, in various ways, imposed his jurisdiction upon the Church which he protected, and not vice versa. The points of reference which can be applied to the Church today are drawn from the period that preceded the decisive events of the 16th century.

In the case of the Pope, one can argue that the advent of the mass media has greatly altered the nature of the sacred and given rise to a new religious phenomenology. Within the Protestant Churches, the role of the preacher has been heightened through television: one need only think of the role which television evangelists have played in the United States. Their influence was decisive not only in the election of Ronald Reagan to the presi-

dency, but also upon the President's public profile and discourse. One of them even tried to win the Republican
nomination for the presidential election of 1988. Pat Robertson
did not manage to progress beyond the primaries, but it is significant that he should have stood as a 'television evangelist'.
Such a situation calls into question, certainly, the distinction
between State and Church, despite the belief of the founding
fathers that such was the great novelty of the American nation at
its inception. Through their discourse, the television evangelists
have reached out to worshippers of every denomination, cutting
across the distinction between Catholics and Protestants. Here
once more the link has been evident between the immediacy of
the message and the personality of the televised messenger. It is
upon the preaching of the messenger, and not upon the printed
word of the Bible, the ultimate repository of the sacred within
the Protestant tradition, that attention has been focused. The
importance of presence has been clearly brought out by television, which has created the forum for an audience to take part
directly in a divine experience mediated through the person of
the charismatic evangelist. The promise of personal prosperity
and recovery from illness have accompanied the preaching of a
message which assured divine intervention in the day-to-day
business of living. Through this supposed association between
a divine presence and the preached word, religion becomes an
object of shared experience which has its place in daily life.

What seems evident today, then, is the diminished role
accorded to the language and trappings of the sacred within
the religious context, and the place which religion has come to
occupy in the day-to-day aspects of social life. Yet the presence
of religion in politics takes other forms from those discussed
above, forms which do not use television directly but which rely
nonetheless upon the existence of the mass media. The role of
the Churches in South Africa is well known throughout the
world. Even the apartheid-supporting stance of the Dutch
Reformed Church, the moral mainstay of the Pretoria régime,
has undergone the modifying influence of other Reformed
Churches, the Catholic Church, and above all the Anglican

Communion personified by Desmond Tutu, Archbishop of Cape Town. The liberation theology which has been formulated by a number of Latin American prelates is also common knowledge, most particularly in Brazil. The result of the latter has been an increase in the role of the secular in the Catholic Church. The Workers' Party of Lula, heavily influenced by this theology, won the elections in São Paulo and is now in a position to contest the next round of elections in Brazil. In a similar though more general way, the role of the Church is evident in Central America, notably in the activities of Romero, the Archbishop of San Salvador, or of Obando y Bravo Archbishop of Managua. Romero's life is particularly interesting, for here we have a bishop of very traditional beliefs and tastes, opposed at first to the Church's intervention in matters that did not directly concern it, converted to the idea that the Church should intervene directly in political affairs.

It can be argued, therefore, that the language of religion is shifting nowadays from the domain of the sacred and becoming increasingly an element in the forging process of history. Within this perspective, the language of politics and the language of religion are becoming ever more closely associated. This serves to refute one of the best known of Gramsci's assertions, the claim that the active participation of the Catholic masses in political process (at the time through the Popular Party of Don Sturzo) would lead them to embrace the class struggle within a wholly Marxist perspective. The language of religion has in fact appropriated the discourse, but not the reasoning, of Marxism.

The language of religion seems capable nowadays, in this post-sacred phase, of opening up new possibilities to political discourse. According to Dietrich Bonhoeffer, a theologian put to death by the Nazis at Flossemburg for his part in von Stauffenberg's plot to assassinate Hitler, God should occupy the very centre, not remain at the periphery, of a secularized social order. (It was a novelty for a Lutheran pastor to embrace a rationale so dear to Catholic reformist theologians, who deemed popular insurrection and tyrannicide, where warranted, to be quite permissible.) To place God at the centre of a secularized society, argued Bonhoeffer, was to necessitate a change in the language by which God was invoked, even to the point of giving expression to the pain, suffering, and abject failure of humankind.

The language of religion, then, tends nowadays to be more directly political, that is, to acknowledge the social transformation that is required alongside conversion as a fundamental element in the religious experience. At the Latin American Episcopal Assembly of the Catholic Church, held at Puebla in 1979, the 'structures of sin' came up for discussion in a way which suggested clear parallels with those structures of society that were seen as the institutionalization of human evil and rank injustice. Though this concept has never been clearly defined, it appeared again in *Sollicitudo Rei socialis*, John-Paul II's encyclical on the question of the North–South divide.

It is by such means that the Church has come to interpret the Third World, though this probably bears no relation to the rapport between Churches and the prevailing social structures of developed countries. The transformation of political structures has become an important part of the whole concept of conversion and evangelization. The uses which are made of such concepts by Churches in the Third World has been contested by the Church of Rome. This shows clearly the tensions and uncertainties which this blend of politics and religion brings about between the upper reaches and the grass-roots of the Catholic Church. It is here that the problematic association between religious discourse on the one hand, and political discourse on the other, is cast in sharpest relief, for the Catholic Church, unlike its Oriental and Protestant counterparts, has, throughout the course of the last thousand years and more, stressed its specifically political role as an institution. Faced with the complexity of the world in an age of technological advance and ecological concern, the discourse of the Church is constrained by the fact that it must carry some political clout without being transformed into a formally recognized protagonist in the political arena, such as a party or a State. It is nonetheless clear that the very real existence of a Church temporal, however negative its connotations, must either lead to direct involvement in the political process or to the invocation of some apocalyptic intervention of God's hand in history.

The term 'millennium', a classic item in the vocabulary of apocalyptic movements, makes its appearance, albeit in a mild guise, in the thought of John-Paul II when he refers to the end of the second Christian millennium. The more catastrophic history becomes, the more God's kingdom approaches. The political language of the Church, which has assured it its place in history, is informed by the notion that the 'ultimate' points of time will be the decisive ones. This represents the conversion of the social and political world to the idea that God's reign is present through history. Within this perspective, the role of charismatic phenomena in the Church—such as healings, speaking in tongues and apparitions—should be evaluated. In the apparitions of Mary there is an impression of immediate presence that appears to transcend any sacred link. The fact that such apparitions (like those of the Virgin Mary at Medjugorje in Yugoslavia) have become daily occurrences shows once again here the link between religious discourse and social presence within an apocalyptic perspective. They remain apocalyptic in their message, announcing God's judgement upon a world history dominated by evil.

As political discourse loses its Utopian thrust, the language of religion assumes an inherently critical attitude towards technological society, exalting the presence of the Church as a liberating force, and anticipating a divine intervention which will save human history from dissolution. The Utopian view of history promises a future that is redeemed by the action of a particular group whose presence alone makes salvation possible: was such not the Utopia of the Communists and the role of the Leninists? The fact is that this perspective has been taken over by the new religious discourse, though the form in which it finds expression now is neither clear nor systematic nor coherent. The transformation of the language of religion into the language of politics has become a source of conflict within the Churches themselves. And yet it is not within the Christian context that the fusion of religious and political discourse, or rather the elevation of the latter to the status of the former, is best exemplified. The real theatre for the confrontation between the religious and the political is the creed within which no distinction between the two has ever been recognized: Islam.

Islam and politics

The Islamic faith is as different from the Christian in its vision of God, man, and the world as it is similar in its fundamental concern with these same questions. The God of the Christians is the God of Mohammed, Jesus is the prophet who precedes Mohammed, the Messiah of the Jews, who failed to recognize him. He was born of the Virgin Mary and died in appearance only. He is therefore still alive and will be present at the Resurrection and Last Judgement. Upon the same fundamental basis, Islam constructed a universe that is wholly different from the Christian. Within the Christian tradition, the message of salvation is a personal one; the Church which is founded upon this message is different from any social or political community. As an organization which claims to serve the will of Christ, the Church acknowledges, even in a limited degree, its autonomy from the State. In a different way from the Catholic Church, the Oriental and Protestant Churches also recognize their separation from the political sphere and, in so doing, acknowledge the legitimacy of the State. There is always present, however, a conflict which centres upon this notion of legitimacy, never more so than in the form of Christianity espoused by the Catholic Church.

In the case of Islam, on the other hand, God's word, while it is addressed to the individual through the intermediary of the prophet, has as its ultimate objective the establishment of a universal community which will order the lives of men in their every aspect. The Koran, unlike the Gospel but in similar fashion to the Hebrew Bible, provided the norm for a community, the *Umma* which was to encompass all Muslims. This community was to be governed by one man, the caliph, chosen from the line of Mohammed's direct descendants. After several centuries, however, in the wake of the great controversy between the Umayyades, the Fatimides, and the Abbassides, the office of the caliph disappeared, with the result that the Muslim world today finds itself bereft of any legitimate authority to govern it. The idea of a wholly unified society with the Koran as its guide, implicit within the Islamic conception of the world, lends an air of illegitimacy to the separate Muslim states. With the exception of Morocco, which insists upon its descendance from Fatima, the other Muslim states have no legitimate basis in Islam. The European powers have created within the Islamic world states on the European model, a model which is defined, historically, within a Christian frame of reference. The difference between Jesus and Mohammed is the difference between Christianity and Islam: the crucified Messiah is very different indeed from the warring prophet, seeking to impose Islam upon the world by force of arms in a holy war, forcing pagans to choose between conversion and death. In this sense, the concept of personal liberty, the right to dissent, and the very idea of individual rights, give way to the concept of an *Umma* that is imposed by force and for which the only rule of law is the word of the Koran. It is for this reason that the Christian ethos, applied to the political plane, is incomprehensible for the Islamic world: the lay State, freedom as an individual right, the autonomous role of the State through its political and legal institutions, can have no place within an Islamic context. It is for this reason that the Arab states which exist today can be seen as a legacy of their colonial past. They would have some point if a coexistence were possible between a secularized Christian world and the Arab community. Any peaceful coexistence however, is made impossible by Christian support for the State of Israel. For Muslims, Palestine is *dâr al-islâme*, the land of Islam where Islamic faith should be practised. Even if the Palestinians were to reach some agreement with Israel, the relinquishment of Islamic land would never be countenanced by Muslims. In Muslim memory, Jerusalem is associated with Andalusia, which was lost in the 15th century and which remains still a painful wound. At bottom, the real problem is not that which divides Palestinians from Israelis, but the religious tensions which exist between Jews and Muslims.

From the fundamental conflict outlined above, a movement of opinion has developed which has been defined as *Islamic fundamentalist* and which holds its chief adversary to be neither the Europeans nor the Israelis, but the nation-based structure of Arab and Islamic states which it considers devoid of legitimacy. These movements, of which the best known came into being in Egypt in the 1920s under the name of the 'Muslim Brothers', have been defined by Maxime Rodinson: they are movements which 'seek to resolve all social and political problems through religion and to re-instate the fundamental principles of dogma'.[1] The definition is too heavily reliant perhaps upon Christian language; but it expresses clearly the desire to make the Koranic law the law of the whole Muslim community, sweeping aside the traditions that have allowed the Muslim *Umma* to be divided into poltically distinct states and the Islamic world to be rent into individual nation-states. Such movements have been defined as 'Islamic fundamentalist'. They seek in fact to distinguish themselves from all of the traditions that have been spawned by the compromise between the *ulama*, the official interpreters of the Koran, and the illegitimate political institutions which have in turn ruled Islam and of which the Arab national states are but the latest manifestation. The notion of an individual Arab state or 'Arab nation' is denounced by the Islamic fundamentalists as a Western corruption of Islamic thought. It comes as no surprise that the ideas of Arab nationhood and Arab nationalism should have been welcomed with such enthusiasm by Christians, who saw therein a means of assuring citizenship within the countries concerned. The impact of the Muslim Brothers was particularly felt in the two states which had been foremost in founding the idea of Arab nationhood and Pan-Arabism: Nasser's Egypt and Assad's Syria. Sadat died at the hands of the Muslim Brothers, even though the group's founder, Hassan al-Banna, had been

---

[1] Cited by Bruno Etienne in *L'Islamisme radical* (Paris: Hachette, 1987), p. 168.

assassinated in Egypt and the movement periodically decimated by Nasser. The persecution of the group in Syria was fierce: approximately 15,000 Muslim Brothers were killed at Hama in 1982. Three years earlier, they had attacked the Military Academy at Alep and massacred the cadets there.

Islamic fundamentalists, too, are children of the mass communications age. Nowadays television is everywhere: 'for the first time, élites must speak the language of the common people, a people schooled in Arabic as never before. There is something milleniarian about this 15th century after Mohammed, the paradox being that it is the people who are obliging their leaders to articulate a millennarian message—a message which, one suspects, they would readily forego—until such time as the initiative passes back into their hands. This will not be achieved until full account has been taken of the evolution, the "Islamization", of Arab civil society, for the Arabic language is indissociably linked to Islam'.[1] The upsurge of Arabic learning in Algeria allowed thousands of teachers linked with the Muslim Brothers to dispatch throughout the country further thousands of teachers who articulated a message quite at odds with the socialist programme of the Algerian government. By 'Arabizing' Algeria, the left-wing government 'Islamized' it, and prepared the way for the day when Algerian universities would be full of students prostrate in prayer before Islam.

The media have made the people prime participants in political discourse and have allowed the formation of a class of intellectuals very different from those produced by Islamic tradition. In this way, a new figure has emerged, that of a preacher re-reading the Koran as though for the first time and investing it with a literal and revolutionary significance. This is at once a fundamentalist renewal and a return to source. Recorded cassettes allow the message to be transmitted beyond the place of worship. There is a short-circuit somewhere between the cultural elevation of the masses, the means of social communication through which this is achieved, and the emergence of popular

[1] Ibid. p. 121.

preachers who argue a link between the needs and the discourse of today's mass society and the letter of the Koran.

What Samir Amin argues in a cultural context of the 'disconnection' between the Third World and the developed countries is daily harped upon by popular Islamic fundamentalist preachers. The countries of the Islamic Third World are increasingly convinced that Western-style development is not to be theirs. They are part of the communications network which such development has spawned, without being able to attain a standard of living in keeping with this. Western development seems impossible for them; that is why they must seek another course. The language of the West has nonetheless permeated the masses of Islam, and the values which it expresses are becoming part of their language. Equality, fraternity, the rights of women, essential freedoms: all have found a place in Islamic discourse: 'The response to allogeneous modernization is ultimately to trade the nationalization of progress for the Islamization of modernity'.[1] The process whereby agricultural traditions are uprooted in the creation of that typically Western establishment, the city, cuts off the masses, in the modern sense of the term, from the fabric and the solidarity of the village, with its oral culture and traditional hierarchy. The new network of social communication creates another sort of community to replace the one which has been abandoned.

It is for this reason that the chief enemy of Islamic fundamentalism is not the West or Zion. The principal targets are the established religious and (above all) political authorities of the Arab states. The fundamentalists are convinced that the fall of Islam and the 'reign of disorder' that now prevails (*jâhîliyya*) result from the infidelity of Muslims towards Islam. Signs of the disorder in question are to be found, it is argued, in the nationalist ideologies of Arab states and in the Islamic *umma's* cultural infiltration by the Christian West, which is still referred to as the 'land of the Crusaders'. In order to halt this reign of disorder, it is necessary to put an end to the westernizing cosmopolitanism

[1] Ibid. p. 132.

which has permeated political thinking in the Arab world. Sadat's assassin yelled that he had murdered Pharaoh. So there is also here an eschatological dimension, a 'coming' or 'revelation' of sorts, the fulfilment of history through the establishment of Islam throughout the world, beginning with the Islamic countries themselves and extending to those places where Islam is in the minority. The official organ of the Organization of the Islamic conference itself, a publication supported by the Arab governments, in particular the Saudis, reminds its readers that Muslim minorities in foreign countries should strive to be an authentic part of the *umma*, to 'succeed' despite their minority status.[1]

It is clear that the fundamentalist interpretation of the Koran encompasses the whole of the Islamic world. The fundamentalist movement was born and developed among the Sunnites. It is therefore wrong to believe that the new political interpretation of the Koran arises from the influence of Khomeini in Iran. The religious hierarchy of the mullahs and the ayatollahs in Iran used the fundamentalist phenomenon for its own ends, as the Sunnite *ulama* found themselves overtaken by new popular preachers. This development owes something to the differences between the Shiite and the Sunnite traditions. In the *sî a*, besides the Koran and the *Hadîth* of Mohammed (that is, the words and acts of the Prophet as transmitted by oral tradition), there are also the writings of the twelve *imâms*, the caliphs who came after him. The doctrine of the hidden *Imâm*, the *Mahdî* who may reveal himself, brings a still stronger eschatological tension to bear. For centuries the Shiite, considered heretics by the Sunnites, had to go underground. The dramatic swelling of their numbers meant that they could at least come out into the open and seek to fulfil the *sî a* as a true Muslim tradition within an Islamic fundamentalist perspective. Khomeini sought to impose Shiite direction upon the whole Islamic movement. In this he failed, even in Lebanon, where the *ulama* have accepted the role of Khomeini not as representative of the hidden *Imâm el Mahdî*,

[1] *L'Islam aujourd'hui* (Rabat, 1983), no. 1, pp. 105 ff.

but as jurisconsult only. Within the Iranian tradition, Khomeini is regarded as the infallible *Imâm*, who will bring his reign of justice to the world.

Khomeini's politics have been an endeavour to translate into reality the fundamentalists' conviction that Arab nationalism is the real enemy which prevents the eschatological realization of the world-embracing *umma*. The same criticism was levelled against Saddam Hussein by the Muslim Brothers. Yet neither the Iraqi Shiites nor the Sunnite fundamentalists endorse Khomeini as their leader. Hundreds of thousands of young lives have been sacrificed to the Iranian *imâm*'s tragic ambition to become the guiding light of Islam in the world. The reduction of Khomeiniism to 'revolution in a single country' weakens the Islamic cause by throwing into relief all of the difficulties by which it is rent.

This does not mean that the fundamentalists have lost their every card. They are, on the contrary, a growing force in all Islamic countries. The rapprochement between the language of religion and the language of politics is nowadays an accepted and commonplace fact. This allows the present moment to be represented as a unique and ultimate point in the historical scheme of things. One might add that apocalyptic tension is also an element in a Western secular culture which is ever more acutely conscious of the tensions between ecology, technology, and demography. It is indeed a significant moment when man has, through his own creative experience, gone beyond the natural boundaries of his history and his environment.

Any attempt to discover an Absolute purpose in the historical process has its dangers, if it is linked to the figure of an omnipotent God. For this reason, the Christian world furnishes, even if in a peripheral way when compared to ecclesiastical institutions, the image of a God who stamps upon man's countenance the pain of creativity. In this sense, the differences between the Christian world and the Islamic world are again sometimes surprisingly evident. All that is new in the Islamic world is not fundamentalist. The mystical tradition is still strong, insisting as it does upon private conversion, the conquest of the individual being seen as the first necessary step in the conquest of the State. The founder of a Turkish brotherhood, Bayyed Ed Din Nursi, declared that he was 'educating himself, learning the modern sciences the better to understand and to implement the ways of God.[1] Turkey, a country with a great mystical tradition, furnishes intellectuals who are far from being militant preachers. They encourage 'personal reflection' as a necessary antidote to the paralysis of 'fifteen centuries of exegesis serving the vested interests of successive rulers'.[2] Here, too, the need for a return to sources is apparent, but in a sense that is quite the opposite of what is preached by the Islamic fundamentalists. It was they who pointed out, in response to Khomeini's *fatwa* condemning Rushdie to death, that a *fatwa* is only valid in an Islamic land.

The future of the world will depend now to a large extent upon the choices made by the Islamic community. The new proximity between the language of religion and the language of politics may be a blessing or a curse upon human destiny. This depends upon religious thought's capacity for self-renewal, and here it is disconcerting to note that, whilst religious *enthusiasm* is on the increase, *thought* is marginalized within the Catholic Church. This marginalization has in fact brought about a crisis within a whole religious current which, fostered by Vatican Council II, is as significant as any ecumenical movement.

[1] *Le Monde*, 13 April 1989.
[2] Ibid.

Islam and the Turkish Community in West Germany: Religion, Identity and Politics

Hamit Bozarslan*

German sociologists choose the term 'ethnic group' to describe the Turkish community in the Federal Republic of Germany. This term is wide enough to indicate both strong, deep-rooted specificities binding together Turkish nationals in West Germany, and also social and political diversity within the Turkish community. An ethnic group is never a uniform mass; the term signifies a community characterized by varied socio-economic conditions and often by varied cultural and political conditions.

Factors influencing the place of religion in the Turkish immigrant community in West Germany

Originally, immigration concerned mainly the Anatolian peasantry. These peasants had never been to the main Turkish cities like Ankara or Istanbul and saw urban life for the first time in Cologne, Munich, or Berlin. For them, Islam remained one of the mainstays of everyday life and formed part of the collective memory. Shocked by the lifestyle of the city-dwellers (which Turkey wanted to adopt), the peasants, 'urbanized' through immigration, turned back to their traditional values based on religious identity, as a means of ensuring the cohesion of the community and the family and as the best antidote to the destructive effects of German urban life. From the beginning, therefore, the conditions in which immigration took place

* Political scientist.

115

helped to establish the central place of Islam in the daily life of immigrants, both as faith and as an expression of identity. To speak of the 'discovery' or 'rediscovery' of Islam by Turkish immigrants in the 1980s is therefore to misunderstand the reality of the situation before 1980.[1]

At the same time, immigration enabled popular Islam, which had been severely repressed during the Kemalist period,[2] to come out of its shell, expand and organize and express itself freely, ironically in the land of the 'Infidels'. In some sections of the Turkish population, Islam emerged as an ideology and as a force for social action and the transformation of Turkish society. The increasing flow of immigrants camouflaged a stream of political exiles, who took with them the message of Islam as an ideological and social force. Over the years, changes in the composition of the migrating workforce led to the creation of commercial networks (grocery shops, wholesalers, and restaurants make up two thirds of these networks today) which provided the economic support necessary to develop large-scale autonomous action and reinforce the ideological message of Islam.[3]

In these already favourable conditions, Islamic movements also had a considerable impact. Whereas their capacity to influence political life in Turkey was initially very limited, they found it much easier to find a place in Islam in 'exile' and even managed to use Germany as a base for spreading their influence in their native country. Later, their increased political influence in Turkey allowed them to strengthen their presence among immigrants.

The battle for dominance of the immigrant community between the various Islamic movements led to deep splits within the religious camp, particularly when a section of Colonel Türkes's 'Grey Wolves' became 'Islamists' during the 1980s and

[1] Reiner Werle and Renate Kreile claim to see a 'rediscovery' of Islam in *Renaissance des Islams: das Beispiel Türkei* (Hanover, Junius Verlag, 1987).

[2] See M. Sencer, *Dinin Turk Toplumuna Etkileri* (Istanbul, Ant Yayinlari, 1969).

[3] See Czarina Wilpert and Ali Gitmez, 'La microsociété des Turcs à Berlin', in *Revue Européenne des Migrations Internationales* Vol.3, no. 1-2, 1987, p. 187.

increased their influence among certain groups such as the *Süleymanci*. The *Süleymanci* emerged victorious from this power struggle, along with other groups such as *Milli Görüs*,[1] the most important Islamic organization among Turkish immigrants in West Germany. *Milli Görüs* has very close ties with Necmeddin Erbakan's Party of Prosperity (*Refah Partisi*). Its propaganda activities are intense and it can mobilize as many as ten thousand people on occasion.[2] It is reckoned today to have a network of eighty associations and 300 places of worship and Koran schools. The *Süleymanci*, who take their name from their spiritual founder Süleyman, have stepped up their activities dramatically in the last few years. Today they boast a network of 210 associations and places of worship, and a total of 18,000 members.[3] Other important groups include the Islamic Union, close to the far right in Turkey, which appears to have around a hundred associations under its control, the *Kaplanci*, whose positions are close to those of the Islamic Revolution in Iran, and a number of smaller groups composed of intellectuals and students. The *Hür-Türk* (associated with the party of the Turkish Prime Minister T. Özal) are accused by the Turkish Islamic organization *Milli Görüs* ('National Vision') of being only 'half Muslim',[4] but, like the former Grey Wolves who became the defenders of Islam, their extreme Turkish nationalism does not prevent them from playing the Islamic card, which confers legitimacy and can be politically useful.

[1] The adjective *milli*, literally 'national', is close to *umma* ('Islamic community') in Turkish Islamic vocabulary.
[2] When Erbakan visited Germany, 10,000 people attended a meeting called by *Milli Görüs*. The group also gathered 3000 people for a conference on 'Problems of Islam in Europe' held in Rotterdam.
[3] This movement, with the tacit support of certain politicians, has grown considerably in Turkey in the last ten years or so. See G. Saylan, *Islamiyet ve Sivaset, Türkiye Örnegi* (Ankara, V. Yayinlari, 1987), pp. 100–104.
[4] U. Muncu, 'Islamci Orgütler ve Para', in *Cumhuriyet*, 1 March 1987.

The Turkish state as an actor on the religious scene

For many years, the Turkish state, despite its view of secularism as a means of ensuring state control over the religious domain and its intention of using immigration to extend sovereignty outside national frontiers, was largely unable to exert control over religious affairs. The state's view of secularism was heavily criticized by Islamic groups in Turkey.[1] But it is outside Turkey (and hence outside the reach of judicial or administrative sanctions) that criticism of the state's control of religious affairs was most radical. This led Ankara in the 1980s to intervene in religious affairs through the directorate of foreign affairs. The foreign affairs directorate, which alone has the right to direct the 'religious affairs' of the 'secular state', has been particularly active since the military 'coup' of 12 September 1980 which adopted the 'Turkish-Islamic synthesis' as official state doctrine. The 'Turkish-Islamic synthesis' combined Turkish nationalism (specific and exclusive to Turkey) with the spirit of the Islamic community (*umma*) and conferred a religious legitimacy on the state. The regime sought thus to regain control of religious affairs, which had been severely shaken in the 1970s, and hoped (in vain) to block any chance of a resurgence of Erbakan's party. Despite cutbacks in funding and staff recruitment in the civil service, the foreign affairs directorate continued to increase in size during the 1980s.[2]

The Turkish state's intervention in religious affairs is thus motivated by the need to regain control and restore the legitimacy of the state. In addition, Ankara has seen that Turkish nationals in foreign countries are receptive to many messages, not only those coming from the Muslim world, but also those coming from the left, whose influence in Turkey is limited to small, clandestine groups. Ankara has therefore pursued a policy aimed at countering these messages and building solid bases

[1] See, for example, I. Özel, *Irtica Elden Gidiyor* (Istanbul, Iklim Yayinlari, 1987).
[2] On the 'Turkish-Islamic synthesis' and the religious policy of the 12 September regime, see G. Saylan, op. cit., pp. 61–67.

within the immigrant community, and has used religion to this end. The legitimacy of the state, embodied in the Consulate and in schools, has thus been reinforced by the increasing number of imams within the Turkish community abroad.

In this way, the state has become a central actor in the process, with infinitely greater means at its disposal than the various Islamic movements (salaries and diplomatic posts available for the imams, for instance). The state has also sought to reinforce its legitimacy and its presence by posing as the defender of the 'one and indivisible' Republic, the Kemalist tradition, and the Muslim faith all at the same time. On these grounds, it has attacked the various Islamic movements for 'trying to destroy the Turkish Republic'.[1]

Nevertheless, although it controls some 300 places of worship today, the foreign affairs directorate still faces stiff competition. The Islamic movements, strongly rooted in the immigrant community, have even infiltrated the foreign affairs directorate itself. For many of them, the directorate represents a usurper state (or merely an elite), an infidel state, belonging at best to the *dar-ul-sulh* (House of Truce, mid-way between the House of War and the House of Islam) but certainly not to the *dar-ul-Islam* (House of Islam, Muslim territory).

Religion: an open field

It is difficult, therefore, to see the religious domain as merely an arm of the Turkish state. On the contrary, it is open to the whole of the Muslim world. Contacts with the Muslim world, whether economic or legal, are made more easily from a European base than from Turkey. In some organizations, Turkish activists work side by side with Syrians, Jordanians, Pakistanis, and Iranians.[2] There is no doubt that contact with these people, because of their history and their militant traditions, has a radicalizing effect on the Turkish activists. In addition, some Muslim states appear

[1] U. Muncu in *Cumhuriyet*, 5 March 1978.
[2] This is true of the Islamic Federation: see U. Muncu, in *Cumhuriyet*, 4 March 1987.

to play a direct role. It seems likely that Iran has close links with the *Cemaleddin Kaplan* group, which advocates nothing less than an Islamic revolution in Turkey. The states of the Arab peninsula are also in contact with some Turkish Islamic organizations and publishing houses.

Turkey, the homeland, and itself a Muslim country, is therefore not the only force of attraction. Moreover, Turkey feels the need to use its influence with moderate Muslim bodies in order to compete with the Islamic groupings. Hence, the Turkish regime has cultivated links with the Saudi *Rabita* in order to finance its army of imams abroad.[1] It hopes in this way to reduce the risks of contacts outside its control.

Religious disunity

The final factor which must be taken into account in our analysis of religion and the Turkish community in West Germany, and one of the major causes of division, is the impact of internal splits. The first generation of Turkish immigrants in West Germany plays a much greater role than, say, the first generation of North African immigrants in France. Far from diminishing the influence of the first generation, the influx of political refugees of various persuasions in the 1980s has in fact reinforced it. It is through the first generation that internal splits and allegiances have a lasting impact. Alignments and divisions in Turkey are much more important than theological differences or differing views of the place of Turks as Muslims in Europe. We have already seen the impact of the power struggle between various Islamic groups and discussed the case of *Milli Görüs* and the *Süleymanci*. The delicate and controversial problem of the Kurds is another factor of divisions. The Kurdish supporters of the *Kaplanci* have forced this group to tackle the Kurdish question and to organize protest demonstrations against the Halabjda massacre in Iraqui Kurdistan; some Kurdish Muslims have gone so far as to create a separate organization in West Germany,

[1] Ibid., 1 March 1987.

the Islamic Union of Kurdistan (Islamischer Verein Kurdistan).[1] The creation of this religious and nationalist group appears to stem from an affirmation of Shafi'ite (Sunni) Islam as well as national aspirations. In the same way, the ultra-Shi'ite Nusairis or Alawites, more than ever excluded from Turkish society by the adoption of the 'Turkish-Islamic synthesis' (based on Turkish nationalism and Sunni Islam), demand the creation of an 'Alawite state of Anatolia' and build up their own separate organizations to this end.

Religion is therefore the arena for splits within Turkey and is itself on the point of cracking under the strain of these divisions. The break-up of religious unity is undoubtedly one of the major signs of the politicization of Islam in West Germany.

Religion and the immigrant community

The above remarks must be put into context, for it would be wrong to conclude that the Turkish immigrant community in West Germany is totally dominated by a highly politicized form of Islam. Nothing could be further from the truth: other factors are at work, such as the integrating effects of German institutions on the younger generations, and depoliticization which characterizes the majority of the community and its non-religious associations.[2] Nor should we underestimate the importance of Turkish membership (limited, but constant) of German political parties, notably the Social-Democrat Party and the Greens,[3] and

[1] Religion played an important role in the Kurdish movement of the early twentieth century. But this new organization is a 'first' in the sense that it is the first non-Marxist Kurdish organization of the last twenty years.

[2] See Peter König, Günter Schultz, *Offene Jugendarbeit mit deutschen und ausländischen Jugendlichen in kommunalen Freizeiteinrichtungen* (Bonn, Verlag Neue Gesellschaft, 1984).

[3] Among Turks in West Germany, the level of participation in associations is quite low. Most of the Turkish associations are non-political and non-religious. According to a survey carried out by Peter König, Günter Schultz and Rita Wessel, only 9.4% of Turkish members of associations join religious groups, 7% political groups: *Situation der ausländischen Arbeitnehmer und ihrer Familienangehörigen in der Bundesrepublik Deutschland* (Bonn, Bundesminister für Arbeit und Sozialordnung, 1986), pp. 446–449.

of other, non-religious political groupings (communist, social-democrat, Kurdish nationalist, etc., which have around 30,000 members, as well as the pro-Özal or pro-Demirel 'liberals'). Moreover, West Germany provides a breeding-ground for the Westernized intelligentsia. For these reasons, Islam must be seen as one of the components of immigrant life, but perhaps not the main one.

It should also be said that, contrary to the apocalyptic vision often presented in the media, the majority of Muslims see Islam as a way of life, a sacred code of moral standards, rather than as a political programme.[1] The religious and political demands of the community often overlap but are not completely identical. Quite clearly, the politicization of Islam does not stem from such demands. Religious campaigns (on various subjects such as religious education, or burial in Muslim graveyards) can reach a large section of the community. But they do not necessarily lead to specific political standpoints. Nor do they exclude secular or non-Islamic political allegiances: immigrants can, for instance, adopt 'modernist-liberal-integrationist', Christian-democrat-type politics without changing their conception of Islam as an expression of identity or questioning the religious demands.[2]

Islam as a force for integration?

As we have seen, divisions within Turkish society have a considerable influence on Islamic politics in West Germany and constitute one of the main factors of religious disunity. However, Islam is also influenced by the immigrant way of life and the social and political institutions of the host country.

This ambiguous condition of dual reference and even dual personality is due to the fact that immigration, rather than trans-planting a stable group of Turks from one country to another,

[1] See Riva Kastoryano, 'Paris-Berlin: politiques d'immigration et modalités d'intégration des familles turques', in R. Leveau, G. Kepel (eds), *Les Musulmans dans la Société Française* (Paris, 1986), p. 161.

[2] This was the case for one of the people interviewed in our research, M. A. Senel: interview carried out in Bonn on 5 June 1989.

united a diverse and scattered people to form a solid, lasting ethnic community in West Germany. This process inevitably led to a greater autonomy in relation to the country of origin and the Turkish state. There are signs—although as yet too few to form definite conclusions—which suggest that some elements of the system of interaction at play in West Germany will influence the direction which the immigrant community and the Islamic movements will take in the future. It is conceivable that the future choices of the immigrant community will be radically different from those of their counterparts in Turkey.

In fact, even now we see changes in the attitude of all the actors involved, in a desire to find forms of expression which are acceptable within the German system. Groups from the opposite ends of the political spectrum work together in the 'immigrant councils' as if it were the most natural thing on earth, and this cooperation gives them a real initiation into democratic politics. As a result, the formerly militant and sectarian groups put themselves forward as organizations created in Germany and refuse to be a mere extension of the 'parent' organization in Turkey.

Religion, too, is affected by this change in attitudes, which we describe under the rather provocative label of 'germanization'. *Milli Görüs* is now preparing to sit on the 'immigrant councils', which will give it a new legitimacy within the community and also a new responsibility within the German political system. The group has also begun to cultivate links with some of the German political parties, which will ensure official recognition and an official place in the system. It is also collaborating with the Turkish Communist Party on questions concerning immigration, since the Communists, *glasnost oblige*, are now ready to work alongside the Islamic organizations, to the great displeasure of the 'radical' left. Many *Milli Görüs* members are demanding the right to vote for immigrants.

In general, the Turkish Islamic movement in West Germany does not undermine the Christian foundations of the country. Few Muslims wish to fight for the transformation of West Germany into a part of *dar-ul-Islam*. Although it wishes for a radical transformation of Turkish society, Islam does not seek to upset things in West Germany and limits its intervention to the defence of religious autonomy. Islam has thus become moderate, even conformist. Politics are carried out on different levels in the two countries. In short, although politicization of Islam is in full swing and has transformed religion into a battleground for the power struggle between the various groupings, Islam is becoming more moderate and, as a force for the political representation of community interests, increasingly ready to flirt with the idea of integration. This paradox, which describes the religious dimension of Turkish immigration in West Germany, effectively signals the creation of an ethnic community.

Future prospects

The changes we have examined do not necessarily mean the end of radical politics. It is likely that radical groups will continue to exist within the German system, and they may even become more active. An increase in the 'structural marginality' described by C. Wilpert,[1] political exclusion (which, in view of the strength of relations between the German political groupings and the community associations, is one of the paradoxes of the German system), xenophobia, a sudden worsening of the political situation in Turkey (which could result in a new wave of refugees), a rise in Islamic movements in the Middle East (which seems increasingly unlikely)—any of these factors could encourage a radicalization of some of the Islamic groups and increase their following.

The future is therefore not certain. However, another set of factors exists, which Turkish Islam in West Germany can draw on to complete the creation of its own identity and its own space, which are both more 'German' than dependent on or subordinate to Turkish society. Even though the economic situation of the immigrant community is not particularly rosy, and

[1] See C. Wilpert, 'Structural Marginality and the Role of Cultural Identity for Migrant Youth', in H. Korte (ed.), *Cultural Identity and Structural Marginalization of Migrant Workers* (Strasbourg, European Science Foundation, 1980), pp. 117–129.

despite the 'structural marginality' which the community suffers, the situation is not ripe for politico-religious messianism. The achievement of the single European market, in which the Islamic associations have some interest, should give them the chance to develop their networks considerably and create favourable conditions for change. Finally, the Federal Republic of Germany is not a secular state like France, and can therefore tolerate more easily the idea of political organization of the Islamic movements and the religious autonomy of the Muslim community. The future path of Islam in West Germany will probably depend on the relative impact of these two sets of factors.

European Dossier

Europe and the Hospital Sector: Need and Necessity

André-Gwenaël Pors *

1992: the magic date that has come to stand for hope and for the future. All economic actors are jockeying for position now that the date has been set; by brushing up their linguistic and legal skills and reviving the old boy networks or setting up new ones, they all hope to steel themselves for this turning point in Europe's history.

Yet this is not the complete picture: certain sectors of the economy cannot honestly claim to be getting ready. Be they indifferent, timid, a lost cause or merely unaware of what is happening around them, 1992 spells neither magic nor hope for them. This may well be because their fields of competence do not fall under the provisions of the Treaty of Rome; or alternatively that they prefer to cling to what they know and understand best.

The hospital sector falls into this second category: whether indifference, protectionism or corporatism lies at the heart of the matter, the sector has proved itself incapable of thinking in terms of a European strategy. The situation is not helped by the fact that none of the European Community (EC) texts—and this includes the Single European Act—actually makes reference to the sector, choosing to remain silent on the whole vital issue of health. However, a close look at what the EC has done to date does unearth a number of initiatives in the field of public health. These would appear to be the product of the strange paradox

* Hospital Director, Nantes, France

of the Europe of the twelve, by which economic forces have been brought to bear on social and public health policy.

The hospital sector as an economic player in its own right has a major role to play in the Europe of 1992. Quite apart from the paradoxes implicit in the drive for economic union, Europe represents an uncontestable challenge for its hospitals.

The paradox of the Europe of the twelve

The EC does not in fact make provision for a common public health policy. The single market is first and foremost about the economy. Technology comes second; social policy a poor third. Last of all comes public health. One would be forgiven for considering this somewhat strange at a time when the media is forever bombarding us with information about the single market of 1992: financial, industrial, and commercial news always seem to be at the top of the agenda, closely followed by political strategy, in turn by technology and education. No sector of any economic import is left untouched.

The lack of progress on public health issues is all the more paradoxical when one stops to consider that public expenditure on the health sector represents between a quarter and a third of the GDP of member states of the EC and that household expenditure on health-related products and services will soon equal expenditure on food (rising to 16% of the household budget within the next 10 years.) 320 million citizens are affected by health issues. Yet still the health system and thereby the hospital sector have never been on the European political agenda.

The paradox is again even more striking given the fact that the changes and improvements that have been introduced in the last twenty years in the rules affecting the health sector and its workers have come about as a result of economic imperatives.

The health sector then, represents a serious financial commitment for each member state of the EC but has only by chance come to feature in single market policy. The policymaking approach to the sector has been piecemeal, thereby denying the health sector a role of its own.

The non-Europe of health

The treaties establishing the European Communities are economic and commercial in their scope, as set down by the founding fathers of the Communities in the light of the lessons of history: the nineteenth century saw the Zollverein customs union of 1834 which took the German states—the Germany of the Prussian empire—towards monetary and political union. The Treaty of Rome is thus faithful to history in setting as its goals economic and social harmony (Article IV) and technological development (Article V). The concept of planning for the provision of adequate public health cover, however, received no mention in this design.

One might nevertheless have cherished the hope that the Single European Act would finally accord the health sector the recognition it deserves. After all, questions of public health and state social protection surely rank too highly amongst the concerns of the citizens of Europe not to receive the closest of attention. Furthermore, the Single European Act—which has raised many hopes while arousing the strongest of criticisms—states as its aim to complete the 'European Single Market' by the 1st January 1993. To achieve this, the Commission has put before the Council a White Paper outlining a precise timetable for the adoption of over 300 measures designed to achieve the completion of the economic union first begun in 1958. Yet still there is no mention of the hospital and health sectors as such, although there are any number of references in the European statute books to decisions, objectives, and regulations relating directly to this sphere of activity. Directives have been adopted, for example, in the following areas:

• the control of health and vetinary services within the framework of the elimination of physical barriers within the Community;

- the freedom of choice of supplier, to apply to public as well as private organizations;
- the gradual removal of legal obstacles to businesses wishing to operate in more than one member state;
- the free movement of goods such as pharmaceutical products;
- an extension of the scope of the rules governing public purchasing;
- the freedom of movement of workers and of members of the professions;
- the creation of a common market for services and insurance.

Given that our health, and particularly hospital, sectors are subject to a whole range of nationally-decreed rules and regulations, the scope for change in the wake of such Community directives is unquestionably large.

Nevertheless, in the directives no reference whatsoever can be found to the health services as an economic actor in its own right, neither via the economic and commercial approach taken towards each of its constituent parts by the Brussels Eurocrats—pharmaceuticals, equipment, technology, regulatory control, supply, and training, to name but a few—nor via the more conceptual approach based on the belief in the right of all to a minimum level of health care. This latter approach has arisen from both public concern over health issues such as the environment and consumer protection, and the 'Health for All' campaigns led by the World Health Organization (targeting the provision of basic care; welfare; contemporary problems such as drugs, alcohol and tobacco addiction; AIDS, etc). This approach may well be relatively far removed from the day-to-day running of public health systems, it nevertheless gains considerable public sympathy as it concerns itself with the well-being of every man and woman. Furthermore, it does not attempt to substitute Community for national decision-making. Even so, the sheer weight of the decision-making process at Community level lays the effectiveness of either approach open to question.

It would not be completely true to say that the Commission

has totally ignored all public health-related issues: at least two of its Directorate-Generals and a number of EC initiatives include health and hospitals within the scope of their activities. Thus D-G V (Employment, Social Affairs and Education) employs specialists in the areas of living and working conditions and health and safety. The health and safety function focuses mainly on public hygiene and preventive health measures and was actually written into the original ECSC and EURATOM treaties. Medical services also fall under the aegis of D-G XII (Science, Research and Development) through the 'Biology' and 'Medical Research' offices. And as the centrepiece of its R&D Framework Programme, the EC has recently launched a 5-year 65 million ECU research programme in the field of medicine and public health.

The Commission does in fact consider that part of its role is to facilitate and encourage member states to coordinate their public health and medical systems by exploiting both their own strengths and the opportunities of a single European area. Thus it has established programmes such as ESPRIT, COMETT, AIM, SCIENCE AND ERASMUS. These schemes allow a number of Directorate-Generals to sponsor projects for the exchange of students, medical staff, and research and training initiatives between member states. Furthermore, these schemes aim to enable interested parties within the health system to take part in EC-wide projects and networks; providing, that is, that the interested parties are kept well-informed.

It is not hard to see that a certain reluctance to tamper with issues of such national sensitivity lies behind much of the Commission's policy in the health and social fields. Nevertheless, alarm bells are ringing at the apparent ease with which the health sector is being approached in such a piecemeal fashion, apparently in order to fit more closely with the demands of economic union and thereby reduced to its potential for learning, innovation and profit. One only has to look to Great Britain for an example of what can happen when a bastion of society—in this case the NHS, which has exisited in its present form since 1945—is subjected to the rigours of the economic imperative.

European integration and the health sector: the economic and administrative dimension

Even if the apparent lack of political will to proceed to European integration in the field of public health policy is real, considerable progress has been made in a number of health-related fields, largely as the result of the gradual elimination of physical barriers and of the coordination that has taken place on an administrative level.

The Single European Act confirms that the overriding goals of the EC are to facilitate economic growth, to raise the level of employment and to improve the standard of living of all the Community's citizens. This goal is enshrined in Article 2 of the ECSC treaty signed in 1951. In setting a predominantly economic agenda, the EC immediately distinguishes itself from the Council of Europe which has lain down a set of far broader objectives. It follows that while the Council of Europe can therefore turn to issues of ethical and general interest, the decision-making bodies of the EC must bend to the often discordant political will of its member states and take action in all aspects of economic life. For is not the European 'homo economicus', when all is said and done? Thus the Community's scope for action has been able to expand to the point where it could propose and win agreement on the Single European Act: an instrument which makes provision for a common European currency, foreign policy, and possibly even public health policy.

But in reality the health sector remains no more than an appendage to economic integration. In the following areas for example, progress towards an integrated European health policy has come about only within the context of a higher economic or administrative goal:

- The freedom of movement of workers; the freedom of establishment and provision of services;
- Medicinal products and medical equipment;
- Health care;
- The impact of economic and industrial progress.

The freedom of movement of workers; the freedom of establishment and provision of services

One of the original aims of the Treaty of Rome was to ensure the freedom of movement of labour and the gradual removal of the barriers to the freedom of establishment (Article 2.) The Council has been bestowed with considerable powers in this domain where it has had the authority to decide on proposals put forward by the Commission (once the latter has consulted with the Economic and Social Council and gained the approval of the European Parliament). Since 1975 this legal framework has been the basis for a set of Commission directives providing for freedom of movement for the medical professions. Directives have been adopted so far for doctors, nurses, dentists, vets, midwives, and pharmacists. Policy-making of this kind has necessarily required the Commission to tackle the whole question of the recognition of national qualifications and of policy on the freedom of establishment for non-salaried activity such as self-employment. The same goes for the freedom to provide services within the EC which also has implications for the whole health sector.

Medicinal products and medical equipment

Although the original Treaties contain no specific reference to this field, it provides for the harmonization of national legal frameworks. This in turn has allowed for the introduction since 1965 of a number of measures which aim to harmonize the laws, regulations, and administrative procedures governing pharmaceutical products in each member state. The underlying principle is the control of access of medicinal products onto the market: all such products require a marketing authorization before being sold in each member state of the Community. More recently, the EC has been prompted to propose new measures which are designed to guarantee the quality, safety, and efficacy of medicinal products. Three types of criteria have been established: analysis, clinical, and toxico-pharmalogical. The main purpose of these specialist directives is to protect public health as well as to create a common market in pharmaceutical products and help the development of the pharmaceutical industry.

Healthcare

In their desire to promote economic union, the authors of the Treaty of Rome did not initally address the issue of healthcare. Yet since the health and safety of the Community's workers is not entirely divorced from its economic well-being, Article 118 of the Treaty of Rome (as well as a number of annexes to the EURATOM and ECSC treaties) made provision for the Commission to promote close cooperation measures pertaining to social security and health and safety at work. It should come as no surprise, therefore, that a number of directives have subsequently been adopted in areas concerning public health: the control of drugs, tobacco and alcohol; the protection of the environment; health and safety at work; the quality of life (for example the integration of the handicapped into society); and the fight against today's most serious diseases such as AIDS and cancer. Finally, tentative agreement has even been reached on the harmonization of certain social security procedures: the E111 is evidence of startling success here.

Medical research

Although the ECSC and EURATOM treaties considered a common policy on research to be a priority, it was not until 1972 that the first programme for European collaborative R&D was launched. This was the year that the Committee for Medical Research and Public Health was set up as an advisory body to the Commission and the Council. To begin with, it was proposed to fit measures into existing Community-wide action programmes tackling themes such as ageing, extra-corporal oxygenation, congenital disease, suicide, and so on. In 1980, however, the Commission decided on a new approach to Community cooperative research through the establishment of its Framework Programmes which have since ensured very real cooperation between member states. The first programme covered the period from 1984–1987 and was worth 4.5 billion ECU. The second, worth 6.5 billion ECU, runs from 1987–1991. Both have focused on the development of preventive medicine, the consequences of an ageing population and on medical research into as yet incurable diseases such as AIDS and cancer. Yet further research programmes also have implications for public health: the Industrial Research programme has, for example, provided generous funding (5.5 million ECU) into biotechnological research.

The impact of economic and industrial progress

All health-related areas are directly affected by the economic progress of the industrialized nations: Community actions in the field of biotechnology cover the agricultural, chemical, and pharmaceutical industries; medical services benefit from the convergence of telecommunications and computer technologies; the managerial and operations staff of health organizations are affected by the globalization of markets for medical, computer, and other equipment. Due to the distinct nature of each member state's health service, we find ourselves in a situation where each unit of each national health system has to manage its own financial and operational affairs: each unit has to deal with the state, insurance companies, and banks on financial matters and with the pharmaceutical and medical instrumentation industries, various laundering and catering services, suppliers of computer equipment, and external laboratories to ensure the smooth running of its operation. The services that can only be provided by these units operating as a whole stand to suffer from the effect of such dissipation of effort.

Other sectors of the social welfare system also fear that the future provision of social protection is under threat from the economic imperative. Some even go so far as to fear for the very health of the patient.

No health sector lobby

The twelve member states of the EC spend between 6 and 10% of their GDP on the health sector; hospitals account for the lion's share and are responsible for around half of all household expenditure on medical care. This begs the question as to how such an important beneficiary of public expenditure has been incapable of forming a powerful economic lobby. The direct consequence has been to turn the sector into ripe pickings for interested parties, be they private-sector financial institutions, industrial corporations, or the state itself. I would like to suggest that this situation is due to three major factors: firstly, hospitals are organizations of extreme complexity; secondly the sector is subject to numerous internal and external constraints and, finally, hospitals suffer from perpetual internal power struggles.

The hospital: a complex, non-commercial undertaking

Hospital and clinic directors can nowadays be heard loudly proclaiming that their institution is a commercial undertaking and should be managed as such. While accepting this claim to a certain degree, one simply has to recognize that hospitals cannot readily be classified within the familiar administration–enterprise divide. Indeed, it is difficult to consider the hospital as a productive unit at all. Whether a hospital is service, or profit-driven, the aim remains the same: to provide the best possible service to its customers. There is no single 'hospital product' but a multitude of intermediary 'products'—hospital beds, surgery, X-rays, and the like—which combine to produce an 'output' such as appendictomies and heart transplants.

We can conclude at this point that the hospital is complex because it is effectively a mosaic of productive units (clinics, labs, radiology units, operating theatres, and so on.) A patient cannot be likened to a secondhand car to which one can attribute a relative value or worth. Hence the intense difficulty encountered by hospital directors—whatever their background—in deciding on a strategy acceptable to and capable of implementation by all.

The internal and external hospital environment: additional factors of complexity.

Taking the internal dimension to begin with, the first point to note is that the factors of production differ from those in a commercial undertaking in several ways. As far as 'capital' is concerned, this is characterized by its heterogeneity. It is a function of, firstly, the variety of hardware employed (medical and computer equipment, property, intermediary products, etc.) and the costs associated with this hardware; secondly, it arises from the presence of medical innovation alongside omnipresent research and the beneficial and reassuring products of technological change. Finally, the inevitable concentration of capital in perishable services is a further source of heterogeneity.

The factor 'labour' is predominant, representing over 70% of a hospital's running costs. It is inelastic—a function of the nature of employment contracts and the need for permanent patient care—and heterogeneous in the variety of tasks and skills required of it.

The external environment is characterized by the bureaucracy of the hospitals' legal framework which tends to curb potential dynamism. The heavy hand of the state may go as far as to forbid unauthorized investment; it nearly always extends to budgetary control, either because a hospital comes under the direct control of the state or because the allocation of funding takes place on a national or regional level.

Even if certain aspects of the hospital sector could realistically be likened to private sector organizations, it is obvious that the sector is nevertheless constrained by its own environment.

The hospital: a breeding ground for power struggles

It is customary to describe hospitals in terms of their medical, patient care, and administrative functions. In so doing we automatically oppose the doctor, the nurse, and the hospital director in the struggle for control. Lest we forget, there are others too: the specialists, the biomedical engineers, the computer scientists, administrators, and architects. The three main functions outlined above exist in all European health systems and at all levels of the hierarchy. So who is legitimately in charge? The doctor who diagnoses and cures, the nurse who administers care, or the director who manages both? Consensus would appear ideal but could paralyse the organization. What one finds is that a different figure emerges in each institution: usually the director, occasionally a doctor, and only rarely a nurse.

Paradoxically, the same three functions are to be found in national- or European-scale professional health associations such as the Hospital Committee of the European Communities, which assembles the national ministries responsible for the hospital sector, and the Permanant Committee of Doctors which represents individuals rather than their organization.

This is a pessimistic view of reality in which the hospital as such has no single identity; hence its difficulty in speaking as one voice on a national and thereby on a European level. This mosaic of power struggles, functions, and areas would therefore appear to be a cause for the fragmentation of the sector in the context of EC policy.

Perhaps this will serve as a lesson to the sector which from now on may strive to catch up and adapt to the challenge of the changes which are still to come. For, unfortunately, while hospital directors have only just caught on to the concept of management techniques, company directors are about to leap from this traditional model, which distinguishes still between technique and the individual, towards the 'strategic-professional' model defined by Alain Touraine according to its two major characteristics: the maximization of the potential of the individual and the adaptation of strategy to technical and individual skill.

Seen in this context, the hospitals' future indeed lies in Europe. The changes taking place in the processes of EC policy-making and in other activities are forcing each economic actor to work to precise objectives via strategies which allow for the flexible use of resources. Broad, large-scale schemes must give way to concrete and well-documented proposals.

Contemporary wisdom concerning the nature of the health sector and its structure is about to be shaken to its foundations. Survival from now on will mean flexibility: only in grasping the real meaning of Europe can the health sector hope for a peaceful transition to the healthcare structures of tomorrow.

Hospitals: towards a European strategy

'January 1993: a West German holding group, already the owner of a large insurance company, several pharmaceutical labs and a medical equipment concern has just taken over a number of private hospitals in the EC. It has offered service contracts to hospitals in difficulty and has undertaken a drastic restructuration of its new acquisitions: it is planning to sack existing staff and replace them with university doctors and researchers; it is overhauling existing equipment and plans to set up high-tech treatment centres for cancer and organ-transplant patients.'

Hospital fiction this may be but on a smaller scale has already become reality. There is no health organization, be it public or private sector, which could resist such an attack. Some would positively welcome such an event for the forced change it would occasion and because it would signal the commercialization of the health sector. Others are more cautious and can be found either attempting to face the threat with the meagre means currently at their disposal or by lapsing into turn-of-the-century style complacency. Yet perhaps we should not find such a scenario so unacceptable as it does, after all, symbolize all that is European: a financial, economic, and commercial challenge.

From now on we must choose. There will evidently be conflict, given the multiple systems of social protection, health planning, and access to health care in the member states of the EC. Hence the urgency to meet the challenge now. This will necessitate a clear identification of the exact nature of the challenge and of the means with which to meet it and survive.

The European challenge

Culture

It is patently unreasonable to expect that twelve different health systems could be harmonized either in the short or medium term; it may even be undesirable to do so. Each health system has evolved over time and is, partially at least, the reflection of a particular set of cultural beliefs. And who would maintain that national or indeed regional culture should give way to uniformity? In fact there has been a revival of the cultural identity question in the face of single market deliberations: so much the better. But the health systems of Europe should beware of the private sector and look within for the seeds of change. As a public sector organization set up to promote the well-being of the individual, the hospital has a central role to play in the broader context of public health: just as the private medical insurance companies have their own strategy for Europe, so must the hospitals produce theirs.

The hospital itself then must play a major role in devising a structure strong enough to resist other economic entities hungry for acquisition while keeping a constant vigil over the well-being of the patient. Above all, the hospital must never lose sight of its vocation when fighting in the jungle of the single market and at the mercy of economic constraints and financial, political, and social lobbies. Let us not forget that Jean Monnet himself said shortly before his death that if he could have started all over again with the construction of Europe, he would have begun with culture. Robert Schuman too tells us that 'what really counts is to bestow Europe with a soul, a political will to serve the human ideal'. We should take heart from this.

Administration

As the stereotype of state bureaucracy, France shall be my scapegoat here in demonstrating what Europe 1992 must not become.

We obviously cannot equate the French and EC administrations: the EC numbers about 25,000 civil servants; France has over 2.2 million. Still, Community rules are just as complex and EC bureaucracy too can at times resemble a Kakfa-esque nightmare. Interested parties need to learn how decisions are made and what the respective roles of the EC institutions are. They need to know who initiates, who decides and who vetoes. In December 1988, the European 'boss of bosses', Karl Gustaf Rotjen, President of the Union of Industry Confederations and the Workers of Europe claimed that 'Decisions affecting our businesses are now made in Brussels; that is where we must make our voice heard'. If it is true, as Jacques Delors would wish, that 80% of national economic and social law is to be decided in Brussels, all economic lobbies need to be in a position to act before, during, and after directives are adopted in order to shape, amend, implement, and exploit them.

The variety of hospitals' activities means that they are directly affected by much of Community policy. It would not merely be regrettable but fatal to wait for tomorrow to prepare for action.

Politics

The reason why health and social protection have for so long been peripheral to the European movement is that the sector has traditionally been the reserve of national policymakers.

Yet health policy is not about allocating resources according to political influence nor about negotiating terms with the trade unions in favour with the government of the day. We are concerned with the future of health systems in tomorrow's Europe. Liberalism, cost, and demand are currently challenging tradition: Italy, Spain, and Great Britain each attest to this.

Uncontestably it is in the interest of all concerned to retain a certain balance between public and private sector characteristics. The remit of the state is to guarantee basic rights in education, training, public service, and social protection and to control the private sector, whereas the role for 'private' enterprise in a hospital is to underwrite the individual's freedom of choice. Doctors should have the freedom to set up practice;

hospitals should be allowed to be set up wherever necessary. Beware, however, of a decline in the standards of service and guard against the use of economic arguments as a selection criteria for the provision of certain services. Any future member of the EC will have to pledge its adherence to the respect of the rights of man and to democratic principles; this does not however rule out the freedom to choose between methodologies. In the health sector, political imperatives set ethical priorities; each cultural zone chooses the structure which suits it best.

Strategy

The hospital cuts no image with its environment despite the fact that it is the largest of local employers and disposes of an enormous budget and customer base. Hospitals require a strategy to define a place for themselves in the health systems of the future.

The strategy should first be defined in local and regional terms. Hospitals may well serve a captive market but there is still work to be done to attract universities and companies into cooperative ventures, to diversify sources of supply and to extend the network of local political personalities, councillors, and health services.

Equally, hospitals must become competitive as no protected market can remain so for ever. Competition is to be found at all levels, between teaching hospitals, between state and private institutions, hospital consultants and GPs, and so on. There are various ways for a hospital to become competitive: via the quality of its staff; its methods and focus; and via the extent of its information and collaborative networks. In creating an image for itself as a high-quality and/or well-known institution, a hospital acquires a cachet which clearly identifies its specific character. In formulating a European strategy, hospitals will effectively be mapping out the shape of healthcare systems to come.

Meeting the challenge

Rather than adopt a futurist and somewhat extreme approach to the ideal European strategy for hospitals, one would do better to refer to the etymological origin of the term 'hospital': the reciprocal right to seek and find shelter with another. It can be argued that technological progress, the gradual harmonization of culture and economic growth have combined to bury this ideal. Europe should rekindle it, beginning with the hospital sector.

The Europe that we would wish to create is faced with the problem of corporatism. This obstacle is fourfold in the hospital world: it operates on a national, professional, financial, and individual level.

Nationalisms

The term corporatism does not, strictly speaking, apply to the state yet it is not far from the mark. For does the state not take refuge behind its borders in the name of protectionism? The completion of the single market may remove physical barriers but cannot eliminate attitudes; these will have to adapt but will not disappear for a long time to come. Corporatism is blatant in the health sector and will remain so for as long as the sector remains peripheral to EC policy-making.

The major example of corporatism in hospitals is in the area of planning. In most member states, this function is heavily regulated on either a central or regional level. In certain cases, the imperative is political or administrative rather than economic or financial; in others it is more flexible.

It is hard to imagine how such national entities could ever achieve a degree of harmony, given that each is anchored in its national historical, cultural, and economic past. As with the harmonization of the social dimension, it is not enough to know how to go about it: political will is required.

Professionalism

In this age of individualism, corporatism rules OK. At the last European elections we saw the rise of apolitical candidates campaigning for a variety of causes (animal rights, for example). In the same way, the weakening of trade union power led to the creation of national lobbies clamouring for rights aligned to their own particular profession. The hospital sector has not been exempt from this phenomenon: witness the damaging effects of the nurses' strike in Great Britain and France and the ongoing struggle of the hospital doctors in Spain.

Even more serious is the corporatism borne of acquired and conflicting rights and privileges. The corporatism of hospital directors, doctors and nurses works against cooperation. Even their professional associations do not work together, preferring to ignore each other's very existence rather than pool their efforts. The same is true of their representation on a European scale—the Association of European Hospital Directors, the Hospital Committee of the EC, and the Permanent Committee of Doctors are all cases in point. In the same way, the plurality of the trade unions within the same profession has led to a dissipation of effort: action is always unilateral and may even be in competition with that of another union.

Individualism is also rife. All these attitudes serve to preclude certain countries from playing any role whatsoever on an international level or even within the International Hospital Federation.

The paymasters

While certain EC countries, for example Denmark, may enjoy a relatively straightforward system of public health funding, the same is true neither of traditionally centralized countries such as France nor of decentralized ones, as in the case of Germany. To each country its own system, hence the basic barrier to an integrated health and social policy for Europe.

The administrators—the paymasters—are at the root of the

problem as they are bound by their inertia to resist change. The inertia may lay with the relevant Ministry or health insurance body obliged to resist change to preserve its very existence; it may also be due to the fragmentation of the system or even to governments whose policy is dictated by the political imperatives of the day.

Individualism

No grand scheme can ever completely do away with envy and personal ambition; the health and social sectors are no exception. Even personal gain can be the sole motivating factor for a given individual. While recognizing the role that individual initiative had to play in the birth of Europe and the fact that Europe must provide benefits to the individual, reducing Europe to personal favours and prestige alone would be most harmful to its future image. Entire institutions too may fall prey to a certain parochialism in their approach to Europe; examples of joining the European bandwagon for other than altruistic reasons do exist.

Still further forms of individualism exist which aggravate the existing differences between the public and the private sectors. In France, large financial groups such as the Compagnie générale des Eaux, Suez, and the Caisse des depôts have attempted to build up large chains of private hospitals experiencing troubled times. In the face of such truly Europe-wide strategies, the public sector has become demoralized, and its masters in certain cases complacent. There are examples of hospitals clubbing together to form a common line of defence, only to disband once the struggle is over. For example, private health associations in the United States have attempted to model a system on the 'Health Maintenance Organization'; cooperative insurance societies have tried to bring about the creation of a legal instrument which would allow them to establish a European base.

We all know that in such cases, Europe is about the survival of the fittest where acquired privilege triumphs over altruism.

The goals of a European hospital strategy

While Europe is not exactly the 'sick child' of social policy, it is nevertheless desirable that the most recent stages of European integration should take firmer action in the areas of social equality and the guarantee of access to health cover. The hospital is partially responsible for ensuring that this happens.

European integration at present gives priority to the regions; this in fact favours the hospital sector. Let us now examine more closely the three main themes of European integration as it is taking place today.

Microeconomics: a hospital strategy for Europe

Europe, for each individual institution, represents, above all, a transnational market of customers, suppliers, labour, rules, and standards; in other words an additional administration. It is not easy for the sector to adapt or to adopt suitable measures. A number of practical suggestions are pertinent at this point:

• Finding out how the EC works: familiarizing oneself with the workings of the organs of the EC before the majority of businessmen get there. There are many information centres to turn to: the various European Centres and press offices and the Commission's General Secretariat will all answer one's questions and provide supporting material (videos, bulletins, seminars, and the like);

• The identification of contacts in the EC institutions and in non-governmental organizations (NGOs). As the NGOs linked to the EC are few and far between it is preferable to make direct contact with the relevant offices of the EC itself. D-G V (Employment, Social Affairs and Education), D-G XII (Science Research and Development) and D-G XIII (Telecommunications, Information Industries and Innovation) all work in the fields of public health, current pathology, medical research, biotechnology and technology. The one NGO that does exist and which deals almost exclusively with the hospital sector in Europe is the Hospital Committee of the European Communi-

ties. This is composed of representatives from hospital institutions or from national associations for the hospital sector. It
has existed since 1967 and carries out its work via two subcom-
mittees known as 'Community Coordination' and 'Planning and
the Economy'. The role of this organization can only grow in
the 1990s;
• Building up a network of European partners. Inevitable initial
difficulties should be overcome if full advantage is taken of the
opportunities for contact on the local, regional, national and
European scale. These range from town-twinning to regional
European liaison officers and to relations with suppliers for
whom one is a favoured client. If the will is there, the network
will snowball. It then becomes a question of maintaining contacts, setting objectives and possibly even defining a structure.
Members could even devise a logo: we have had 'European
Villages', why not 'European Hospitals'?;
• The exchange of information and the need to keep up to date.
Being the first with the facts is one of the secrets of success. It
is a question of speeding up the flow of information, making
it easier to understand and making changes accordingly while
keeping abreast of the evolution of others. One way is to plug
into existing networks which, for example, already organize the
regular exchange of doctors, researchers, paramedical, and
managerial staff. Exchange visits can lead to life-long links. One
good example of such a scheme is the 'Young Hospital Admini-
strator' programme which for the last nine years has offered
administrators the opportunity to spend two months observing
the health system of another member state. So in June 1988, a
group went to Nantes and in 1989 to Salamanca. During each
visit, the group holds workshops on themes such as the value of
such visits, the organization and management of hospitals in
Europe, information networks for the hospital sector and the
single market. In a similar vein, the Council of Europe makes
available a number of travel grants to members of the health
services. Such schemes should prove invaluable for European
integration.

'Going European' is not about prestige or mere tourism. It is about defining the hospital environment, developing resistance to competition from all quarters, exploiting new experiences and being proactive. But this is not all: it involves keeping others concerned perfectly informed.

Sustaining and publicizing the strategy

Defining a strategy is the first step. Sustaining it and making it known is the next. Below are three areas requiring urgent attention.

1. Statistical date. There does still not exist any one reliable source of statistical hospital data on a European scale. EURO-STAT has nothing on the subject; neither do the European Parliament information sources. The Council of Health Ministers rarely meets and has not broached the subject. The OECD and the WHO do provide some figures but these are largely inaccurate. A first step to fill the gap would be to organize an EC-wide review of current sources and then to set up an organization to monitor the collection of such data; such an operation could be integrated with EUROSTAT.

2. The Council of Health Ministers. It may come as some surprise that the Ministers for Health of the member states very rarely meet in Council. This may change with progress on the Social Charter, and so it must for without political will there can be no progress. They need to meet to discuss current issues but also to plan for the future. One step they could take would be to set up a separate D-G for 'Health and Social Affairs' and thus demonstrate the political backing to synergy in the health and social fields.

3. The lack of a health lobby. The need to respond to the European challenge should be able to overcome the political, professional and commercial obstacles to the formation of a lobby as well as dispel any hesitation on the part of the International Hospital Federation or the Hospital Committee. There are over 500 associations and 3000 agents lobbying in the corridors of the Berlaymont building in Brussels for business, agriculture,

and the community. The health sector is hamstrung by its own fragmentation at all levels. Diversity can be a strength, and moves are currently being developed to maintain it, for example at a linguistic level. But it needs to be organized. Steps such as the creation of the new 'European Association for Young Health Managers' are vital in order to breed a new generation of managers independent from all forms of political, social, or economic pressure. The future managers of Europe's health systems must be free to exploit Europe's rich cultural diversity in the creation of a superior health system in their own nation or region.

Towards a conclusion

1992 may not herald immediate and drastic consequences for the hospital sector. It is nonetheless a red alert. Hospitals, as the backbone of Europe's health system, cannot afford to be passive onlookers of European integration. They must take a qualitative leap forward.

On a microeconomic level, each hospital must strive towards internal consensus in order to be able to operate on an equal footing with other economic and social actors when defending its interests.

On the local and regional levels, the hospital has a role to play in the health system at large. It can contribute to developments in healthcare provision such as homecare, hospital stay and treatment centres, and outpatient care. It can pool its state of the art knowledge with those responsible for raising the public awareness of health issues.

Each hospital should seek to be at the centre of a network of exchanges aiming at the exploitation of the best that all twelve member states have to offer in healthcare.

The world contains too many examples of bankrupt or corrupt healthcare systems. Europe's cultural tradition is based on the primacy of the individual. The hospital sector must be no exception: it must represent a haven of care for its citizens. Economic integration must not come to mean only the free movement of goods, services, capital, and people but rather the expression of its citizens' well-being and thus health.

We cannot predict the face of the health structures of Europe of the twenty-first century as these will largely depend on the framework chosen by the politicians—the free market, a minimum obligatory legal framework, or consensus. We can, however, confidently predict certain trends: the absolute necessity to curb abuse of the health services; the maintaining of the right level of technological and medical research in increasingly specialized centres; the spread of alternatives to hospital stay; the redefining of the relationship with the patient, the creation of centres of excellence and the limitation of the number of teaching hospitals.

There are now only ten years left before the year 2000. Let us ensure that we guarantee the health of the Community's citizens and thereby of the Community itself.

Europe Now

Democratizing Europe

Enrique Baron

Enrique Baron—who is also a member of our editorial board—was elected President of the European Parliament in July 1989. In an interview with Sami Nair he talks about how he intends to treat his period in office.

SAMI NAIR: *What is the broad outline of your policy during the legislative period for which you have been elected?*

ENRIQUE BARON: First of all I would like to say that the president of Parliament is not a head of government. I say this because one tends to see the President of the European Parliament as being 'above' a normal parliamentary leader, given that his is the highest elected office in the Community. It is the case now, however, that with the developments in the Community, the President cannot simply represent the institution, but must play an active role.

There are two aspects to our work. First of all there is the traditional legislative aspect, and this has still not become completely accepted in the Community. For the moment our main task is to finish the legislative 'package' related to 1992. We are at the moment halfway through the process that was agreed to by our national governments concerning the 300 directives that refer to the economic and social aspects of 1992. The Parliament legislates but does not actually initiate the legislation itself. Most of the Members of Parliament are preoccupied with ensuring that the 1992 legislative package is a balanced one. And there is, of course, a political clash between those who see Europe as

155

basically a free trade area and those for whom Europe must become an organised civil society.

This week, the Parliament declared itself once again in favour of the balanced development of the Single Act. What is meant by that is not just the creation of the single market, but also the creation of real economic and social cohesion, to which must be added today the problems of the environment, technological research, and, of course, the Community's foreign policy, international political cooperation, and European citizenship. The Parliament is addressing all of this in its legislative work.

In the second group of problems I have just mentioned, the Parliament has a reduced legislative power and operates with a very complicated procedure involving two readings and an absolute majority for all amendments. This is a rather draconian situation given that an absolute majority is normally only required in a national parliament to elect a Prime Minister or agree the broad policy outline. Nevertheless, it is true that since 1987, the Parliament has been able to modify bills. And this point is worth stressing. For example, it is Parliament which has strengthened the anti-pollution legislation, extending it to 1400ccs—the 'Californian' norm. The Parliament went further than both the Commission and the Council over the audiovisual issue, when it insisted that the majority of television broadcasting be of European origin. Again, it was the Parliament, in the framework of an agreed protocol with Israel, which has enabled Palestinian farmers to export directly to the EC. Our scope for effective action is wider than is assumed.

The second aspect of our task concerns democratic control, that is, that those who take executive decisions in the Community be responsible to an elected parliament. We have to remember that we have a dual executive; the Commission makes proposals and applies decisions, while the Council, in the final analysis, has both legislative and executive power.

In this parliamentary term we have also come back to the discussion, in a more systematic way, of the question of the broad policy issues of the Community. We have just concluded a debate on the economic and social aspects of the Community, and we shall soon have debates on economic monetary union and on the Community's insitutions. There is also a lot of work to be done aimed at bringing under proper control the extremely complex machinery of the decision-making network of both national and Community bureaucracies.

The Parliament puts great emphasis on the development of the Community as a parliamentary democracy. As I stressed in my inaugural address, what unites us from the political point of view, a Community which includes six republics, a Grand-Duchy, and five monarchies, is that we all believe in parliamentary democracy. And when we speak of the 'common European house', that house is parliamentary democracy. This is why we watch with enormous interest what is happening in Poland, Hungary, the Soviet Union, and so on.

It was the European Parliament which, in the middle of the 1980s, restarted the process of European construction, with the constitutional proposal and Altierro Spinilli's European Union bill. The Single Act was a response to this, and Parliament has exploited the opportunities provided by the act as much as possible. It is, however, a dialectical and evolutionary process. This was what was behind the Council's communiqué, for example, at the Madrid summit which called for reflection upon post-1992 and the respective roles of the Community institutions. The Parliament applauded this proposal by the Council and is ready to join in such reflection in the context of the inter-governmental conference on economic and monetary union decided at Madrid. It would be counter-productive and unacceptable *vis-à-vis* the citizens of Europe to spend our seven weeks in full session speaking only of things like the prototypes of tractors! We must discuss, above all, the way we are to organize the Community democratically, especially the central issues of finance and defence.

SN: *How should, in your view, the often confrontational relationship between the Parliament and the real 'government', that is to say, the Commission, be improved?*

EB: The Commission is not a real government, yet it is one in embryo. The Commission has the right to propose legislation, it is an extremely efficient secretariat, and the relationship between the Commission and the Parliament is based upon what we call in Spanish *'la querencia'* (attraction). We can say that the Parliament wants a Commission that will be a government and vice versa, and it is for this reason that there is now an annual debate in Parliament at the moment of the investiture of the President of the Commission.

SN: *Do you think that one day the investiture of the President of the Commission will be by the Parliament?*

EB: I think that in this parliamentary term, we must establish a procedure by which it can give powers to the Commission, in agreement with the Council. There will have to be innovative changes, but things are possible. The Community rests upon a dual political legitimacy. Sometimes it is too easily said that the Council blocks everything; we have to remember that the Council represents national legitimacies which correspond to electoral majorities in each country. There is also a Community legitimacy which is represented by both the Parliament and the Commission. This legitimacy is not a pure one, and can be criticized on the basis that there is no European electoral law, only simultaneous elections. The Commission is a college whose members must be independent from their government, even though they are appointed by their respective governments, and can be removed from office by them. At the time of the last renewal of the Commission, all the governments except one *proposed* commissioners; one government—Great Britain—*let it be known* that it had appointed a commissioner. There is an important nuance here. Delors and Handrinen were unanimously reelected after consultation with the enlarged Parliament office. This is a positive thing because there was at least some consultation. We should, however, go the next step, and I do not believe it will be so difficult to achieve.

Many today speak of the idea of creating a Senate. This is not, in fact, a new idea; the Dutch put forward this view in the 1950s. Today, people as different from one another as Socialists and Mr Heseltine, the former British Defence Minister, take the idea seriously. In his recent book, Mr Heseltine puts forward a view I can easily agree with: if we create a senate with 76 seats, we would have a perfect bicameral system with members who would be, as the Germans say, the plenipotentiaries of the member-states in the Council.

There could be a bicameral system with a balanced number of votes which could appoint the Commission. Why not? Of course I make this proposal on a purely personal basis. Nevertheless, it seems clear to me that in this parliamentary term, we cannot appoint the Commission in the way we have done up till now.

I define the building of Europe as a 'constitutive' process that has been going on since 1950. You can see this in all our regulations and declarations. Think of the Treaty of Rome, the Coal and Steel Community, the Euratom Treaty, the Single Act, even the Luxemburg compromise which allowed us to get over the 'empty chair' problem created by de Gaulle—a compromise which never had a juridical reality but which nevertheless shaped the life of the Community. These texts were adapted—we should not forget that—by all our national partners, and we can consider them as 'pieces' of a constitution, as it were. There are other pieces too which add to the overall framework. And in this developing overall constitutional framework we are at present developing a political practice that I think is extremely positive, when, for example, we make inter-institutional declarations signed and formally ratified by the three institutions. We did this over the question of racism and xenophobia in 1986, then on the question of the budgetary 'truce' in 1988—a major advance after the war of position which had lasted for so many years. There was also the inter-institutional agreement over the financing of the Community until 1992, and in 1989 we signed an inter-institutional agreement concerning the rights of petition of Community citizens. All these elements have a cumulative effect and are beginning to take on a constitutional value. That is why I have always believed that the Social Charter should not simply be a Council declaration; it should also, in my view, be a declaration which has a constitutional status.

We must, therefore, develop this constitutional process. I think our work at the moment should be one of tuning the engine, as it were, by ensuring, in particular, that our institutions work as democratically as those in our respective countries.

SN: *The European Parliament is clearly not the expression of a state sovereignty, but that of a popular European will—the will, at least, of various democratic European countries. There is, however, is there not, a problem which is not only a technical problem but a legal one: how can you reconcile this popular European sovereignty, expressed via universal sufferage, with that of the different governments? In other words, how can you reconcile the power of the European Parliament with that of the various national governments?*

EB: That is the central question, in fact, and there is a whole theoretical debate around this question going on at the present time. It began in 1948 at the Congress of the European Movement, between the out and out federalists who called themselves Unionists, and the 'functionalists' like Monnet. The Schumann declaration in May 1950 said that progress was necessary via a policy of solidarity, that is, towards federation. We are, in fact, involved in a process of European *union* (and I use the term as it was used, accepted and ratified by all our partners in the Single Act). Union is, therefore, our political objective. What we have not done is define the form of that union. This process is taking place between twelve countries, some of which we should remember—France, Great Britain, Spain, Portugal—are some of the oldest nation-states in the world. Other European nations are of more recent origin even though they express vast historical and cultural realities—Germany and Italy, in particular. So, when we say that the nation state will be transcended, as a quasi-sacred jacobin or paternalistic form, that does not mean to say that this will lead to the dissolution of the nation states. What we have done is to agree to go one stage further than those who governed Europe in the nineteenth century: for fifty years there was the Holy Alliance which apparently operated with total agreement, and this due to the overall hegemony of two empires, represented by such people as Metternich and Castlereagh. Since 1950, the Community has been able to take decisions on the majority principle but be accepted by everyone. This is how the Commission and the Council operate, at least as far as the internal market goes (even though there have been some exceptions), and this is also how the Parliament functions.

What is our relationship to the national parliaments? We are at the present time in a paradoxical yet fascinating period. Because of what was decided in 1957 and is now incarnated in the legislative 'package' I referred to earlier, we are, in fact, taking many decisions. In, for example, the 300 directives that we are at present looking at, there are many major decisions being taken—voting rights at local elections, the position of the young and senior citizens in the Community, audiovisual questions, and decisions concerning capital movements, for example. There are also decisions which may be seen as less important, but, in fact, are extremely significant; for example, the harmonization of norms may seem somewhat absurd at times, but involves billions of ECU. Take, for example, the tractor I spoke of earlier, or of the acceptable noise levels of lawn mowers. In my country, Spain, many norms have traditionally been decided by provincial bodies or by regional governments, but now they become European norms. In certain countries like Denmark, where people are very practical, questions such as pollution or safety at work are considered extremely important. In the Latin countries, on the other hand, we speak a lot about social policies, but we have a workplace accident rate which is enormous compared to those other countries where they do not make great speeches but where people are much better protected by concrete measures.

In many domains, national parliaments are having their powers taken from them, and by a process that is not easily identifiable. What are the implications of these Community regulations and directives for the laws of the different states? National governments can either reinforce Community texts with laws, or avoid legislating on these issues, or else pass laws that contradict Community legislation. This last scenario is a possibility—in fact, has already happened. There are four problems here: on the one hand, there is the process of the assimilation of Community laws into the legal systems in each country, and this is a real problem. It is true that in the Parliament we are going forward at a pace that national governments have difficulty keeping up with; out of 130 directives so far adopted, only seven are law in all of the Community countries. On the other hand, there is the development of regulations. And these have enormous significance. One Spanish politician has remarked: you go ahead and make the laws, just leave the regulations to me. The relationship between Community law and national law is, therefore, problematic, in part because the procedures in each country are often so different.

What can be done about this? The Commission was right to wake us up to the problem, but the allotted time is very limited. On the one hand we have to rely on the general desire to move forward, yet we still have to bring before the Court of Justice the governments that are the least willing to apply Community law or which apply norms that contradict those of the Community. It is somewhat surprising to learn from the official statistics that the best boys in the class from this point of view are Denmark and . . . Great Britain.

To come back to the question of national parliaments, there has been progress. Even a few years ago it was extremely difficult for the Parliament to bring together the Commission and national heads of government. Now it is a regular occurrence. There is now, however, a kind of traffic jam, because we have been, in fact, going far too fast in terms of the national governments' ability to assimilate Community initiatives, we are even going too quickly for the experts. Last year, for example, I was entrusted by the Parliament to organize a conference with Mrs Veil, a kind of Community brains-trust. There were scientists and political scientists from all over Europe and the US.

We realized, however, that universal experts from two continents could not really help us very much. We had to change the organization of the conference to allow journalists and politicians to contribute alongside the academics.

The problem is that we are trying to understand a process that is unfolding extremely fast, and getting ready for 1992 has its rather chaotic side. And the closer we get to 1992, the faster the process becomes. The national parliaments have been stripped of quite a lot of their functions by a process that the parliaments have themselves agreed to. We must understand, however, that this is not a contest between the national parliaments and the European Parliament. That is why we say that in terms of the European Parliament there is a 'democratic deficit' to make up. One of the consequences of what we have freely done, that is increase Community powers in certain areas, is that our national governments are no longer subject to control in terms of what they do at the Community level and even, in part, at the national level. We are trying to ensure, in fact, that governments and, above all, the upper civil service, do not have too much power.

SN: *There is something very new in that. How do the parliamentary traditions of each country inform the European Parliament? What kind of parliamentary practice is emerging from these influences?*

EB: This is an extremely interesting development. I have not been a member of the European Parliament since its creation but I have tried to understand how we got to the stage we are at. What surprises many people is that we work in nine languages. And we can debate and work in all of these languages. It is, of course, a complicated process; over half of our staff are engaged in interpretation and translation, and this takes up over half our budget. Some people dream of creating a kind of new Esperanto, but I think, on the contrary, the fact that anyone can express themselves in their own language and in their own way helps us build Europe. It is often likened to a tower of Babel, and some feel that there should be dominant languages in the Community which would reflect the hierarchy which has *de facto* established itself. But my own view is that we can do at the European level what the Swiss have been doing at the national level since the beginning of the century. For certain peoples, the defence of collective identity inside the Community is extremely important, and this should be stressed.

At the level of parliamentary practice, there are two great traditions: the tradition of British parliamentarianism, which is incremental, with very direct debate, and the continental tradition of legislative parliamentarianism. We, in fact, are creating a hybrid form through a process of interaction. The British bring us the tradition, very dear to them, of Question Time which is not considered very important by many continental deputies, and participation at question times varies significantly according to the different nationalities. Another custom the British hold dear is the emergency debate, that is, topical debates which often involve right–left clashes, and where one can identify majorities very clearly. These often involve questions which take us away sometimes from European affairs (the situation in the Lebanon, for example) but which give to the European Parliament a certain status concerning subjects such as human rights.

What was a strictly consultative task has become a fully legislative one which we welcome totally. In this 518-seat Parliament, a majority, approximately 350, participate actively in the Parliament and this in spite of an awful lot of travelling. On the whole, the deputies are extremely committed to their work related to the Single Act. It is true that we have one very strict rule: a deputy who is absent for more than half of the sessions in the year loses his or her secretarial support. It is a hard system which, nevertheless, encourages commitment.

In this parliamentary session there is in the hemicycle a former President of the Republic, former Prime Ministers—one French, one Italian, one Belgian, many former ministers and European Commissioners—in a word, there are many experienced political figures who are beginning to enter decisively into affairs at the European level. We are witnessing the creation of a European political class which maintains simultaneously its commitments at the national level.

SN: *There is then an intermingling of the two great parliamentary traditions?*

EB: There is no doubt about that. And it is a very welcome development, even though it involves a lot of effort, and the continuous revision and application of regulations. Presiding this Parliament reminds me of the work of those Romans who drove ten-horse chariots. And our own horses sometimes tear off in all directions. There are lively debates on subjects. One has to proceed with great tact, and be able to understand the 'temperature' of the place. The ambiance is sometimes that of the theatre, even of the corrida.

SN: *The European Parliament reflects also two political dimensions: national politics and party politics. Is there a collusion between these? To put it bluntly, do not votes and attitudes sometimes reflect the national rather than the party-political loyalties?*

EB: I believe that the European Parliament is for us like going back to school; the deputies born after the beginning of the European experiment are still in a minority. We are going through a kind of reeducation; we sit down with yesterday's enemies. Today, during a debate, someone paid hommage to Mrs Veil, who had lived in a concentration camp. We also have among us former SS officers. It is important to meet together.

We have a rule: national groups are forbidden. For example, one cannot elect a Vice-president on the basis of his or her nationality. I am in complete agreement with this principle. The multi-nationality of groups is built into the system: in order to constitute a parliamentary group, there must be 12 deputies if three or more countries are involved; if only one country is involved, 23 deputies are needed. Parliamentary groups create both the identity and the policies of the Community. Yet one of our problems is that we talk a lot about building Europe but not enough about who will be the protagonists in this Europe, the people who will live in the house—who will be the political, trade union, and business actors at the European level.

It is a fact that nationally-based political discourse is practically non-existent in the Parliament. There are sometimes MEPs of one country who attack each other along the lines of 'I am a London MEP and our city has no health service'; its fun, it livens things up. But there is practically no national discourse, even commentaries on what is happening at home, in one's country or home region. It is not done.

SN: *You speak of discourse. What about the facts?*

EB: In my experience, inside the large political families, especially among the Socialists and Christian Democrats, MEPs, usually at least 70% of them, vote together on European decisions. I cite these two groups because they are both made up of representatives of a wide spectrum of countries. The Socialist group is the only one where 12 countries are represented, the Christian Democrats represent 10 countries. The Liberal group is much less organized, not, in my view, because of national divisions but because of its very nature.

It cannot be denied that at certain moments the Community divides up and falls back into its national divisions. In spite of the discipline of the groups, there are always the independents within them. There is a category of French independents, for example, on issues such as the Common Agricultural Policy, nuclear weapons, or Polynesia. The British left regularly breaks ranks with the Socialist group over the CAP. The European Democrat group was split in the last session, between the Spanish and the British, over social policy. These cases, however, are the exception rather than the rule. And such behaviour is not highly thought of in the Parliament.

Having said that, one has to admit that tensions remain: tensions which result from the fact that we were all brought up to believe that our neighbours were our enemies.

sn: *Is there a national tradition which predominates, the French or German, for example?*

eb: No. One could, of course, identify certain nuances in terms of daily political life. At the beginning of the year, for example, the French claimed that it was unfair that the two main parliamentary groups were led by Germans. They were, indeed, both Germans, but there was, of course, no collusion, it was just the way these things worked out. It was just that both Germans were extremely well informed and had done their homework.

There is another interesting situation: we cannot say that the enlarged office where the presidents of the parliamentary groups sit is a 'French' office, but it is true that of the ten present group presidents, five are French. People know this, but I have not heard any complaint of a French invasion.

sn: *Let us go back, if we may, to the problem of sovereignty. There is a highly complex structure: the Parliament, the Commission, the Council, the Court of Justice; new forms of sovereignty are being established. In your view, are we heading towards a European state and, if not, what type of system are we heading towards? Is it a federal structure? And if so, is it a federalism based upon the US model, or are we creating something original, a state which does not conform to pre-conceived models?*

eb: The process we are engaged in is of a federalist type, but the road we are taking is hard to define. There is a host of tendencies. There are, for example, the 'hard federalists' who think that all our problems arise from the fact that we have still not created a federation. This view is shared by many people, and is clearly expressed by Mr Maartens. But it is possible that we are, in fact, moving almost imperceptibly towards federation. Our objectives are becoming more and more clearly federalist ones. As for models, we should, of course, take advantage of the best of the US and Swiss examples. Mind you, the European system sometimes resembles more the Venetian republic, the 'Serenissima', through its love of intrigue!

Who would have thought after the conflicts of the nineteenth and twentieth centuries, that republicans and monarchists could work together? Certain countries, like my own, with its civil war, have been open wounds for a long time. We are creating in spite of all that, an original federalism.

It is also worth pointing out that if one analyses the cases of Switzerland and the US, we see that both were very slow historical processes. We, in fact, are going faster. But I, personally, am still not complacent: Europe cannot afford to lose its opportunity. It has to do it properly and in a very short space of time. Nevertheless, I do not want to take a position in terms of models, which involves meticulous historical analysis. For me, it is a question of direction, the movement of history, which matters.

SN: *Even so, I know you are a convinced federalist.*

EB: Yes, In my own country, I have worked a great deal for a solution which would give greater autonomy to the various peoples who feel they are crushed by an over-centralized state. It is an extremely interesting experiment in Spanish terms, and I am convinced that it will end up one day as a federal system.

SN: *There is an important problem in this debate about federations and confederations: behind it lies the idea that national states must prevail in a certain number of areas: one often speaks of defence, foreign affairs, the broad economic orientations, areas where the European Parliament does not carry much weight.*

EB: The national states must continue to dominate on all questions which are not common to all the countries. One often has to explain to those worried by Europe that municipal life, regional life, and many of the functions of the state will remain. But when you speak of defence and of foreign affairs and state perogratives, I hesitate to agree. Five or ten years ago, who spoke of foreign affairs in the European Parliament? It was almost taboo. If I am not mistaken, cooperation in foreign affairs began with the Falklands War in 1982. Now we have the European

'troika' which goes all over the world—the minister, his predecessor, and successor—and the Community is able to formulate
common views on problems as complex as the Middle East,
Central America, and relations with the East and with China.

Defence was a controversial subject when I arrived here four
years ago. But more and more, these problems are discussed and
views taken on them. One even is used now to hearing critical
voices who claim that we are not active enough in this area. More
and more people are convinced that we need a Community view
which is not dominated by the bilateral terms of the US–USSR
debate.

In the medium term, perhaps in the short term, we are faced
with the problem of burden sharing with the US over the defence
budget. This question involves not only American concern over
the question of the budget itself, but also a historical tendency
that is forcing them to reformulate their policies *vis-à-vis* Europe,
and this is happening. The allusion in the Single Act to the
industrial and economic aspects of defence are extremely significant in this respect.

SN: *I should like finally to address the question of the location of
the European Parliament. If it has to go to Brussels, how can
Strasbourg be compensated?*

EB: I agree with the Parliament's view which is expressed in the
Prag Report and was approved by a majority in the European
Parliament. The Report supports the idea of a single site for the
Parliament and for the Community's institutions. The Parliament itself must not enter into a quarrel over cities, but it seems
to me logical that it works as close as possible to the Commission
and the Council in the name of both democratic control and
coordination. A federal system is one of conflictual cooperation.
We welcome coordination between the insitutions, and we practise it: there are many examples of this each month. We also
need a rationalization of our personnel and the services provided
to MEPs.

SN: *But does anyone envisage compensation for a removal of the site of Parliament?*

EB: Everything is negotiable, but this discussion is at present being dealt with by the Council.

Literary Chronicle

Peace, Power and Literature

Siegfried Lenz*

To the limits of peace

As far as the subject of peace is concerned, all of us have a right to express our opinion. Everyone has a dream, everyone is involved; everyone who cares about peace has the right to express an opinion, and so has everyone who has suffered, for suffering is a sufficient warrant. I have no desire at all to challenge the competence of the great masters of politics in this matter—but we cannot grant them a monopoly of the right to work for peace. History has taught us to demand our own right to intervene and our right to speak out—and that means to act—whenever we see peace being threatened. For peace is always threatened, always under attack, in both the general and the specific. From the Old Testament prophets to those Cassandras of our own time who have talked themselves hoarse, there has never been a time when the ideal and the objective of peace were free from attack. Nor has there ever been a time when in the face of such an obvious threat, reason could avoid the responsibility of response—through a visionary programme or a utopia. The New Man, whose arrival has been so often proclaimed—Man who is peaceful, good, conflict free—has never yet appeared, and it is easy to see that we will never meet him. Obliged as we are to live with problems that have no solution, it seems also that we must be content with a peace that is always

* Siegfried Lenz won the German Bookseller Publisher Peace Prize in 1988. The prize is awarded to writers, philosophers and scientists who work for peace. It is the most prestigious prize in the Federal Republic.

173

imperfect—and thus we need not simply to be conscious of that fact but also, in so far as it is possible, to take the appropriate action. Peace can be conceived from a conceptual, philosophical, or idealist perspective and it can be studied and analysed in all its dimensions and conditions. Yet the very fact that peace is incomplete even where it exists means that it will always remain an unrealized goal.

As a writer myself, I am fully aware that literature does not count for much, that its action has been, and remains, weak and intangible. There has never been a time when writing was able to dissuade the powerful of this world from engaging in a war on which they had decided; no work of literary imagination that has ever been capable on its own of abolishing torture or saving children from hunger any more effectively than it could protect the right to freedom of thought. Literature has been wholly unable to prevent millions of people living below the limits of poverty or to save us from imprisonment at the hands of monstrous bureaucrats or from the hopeless contemplation of the death of our planet. Above all, literature has proved incapable of guaranteeing the preeminence of the agency which all peace specialists see as central to the resolution of conflict, namely, human reason. Clearly, the tangible influence of literature is minimal and the writer of today, whose actions always reflect a form of legitimate defence, has reason to be discouraged; the balance sheet of his disappointed hopes obliges him to recognise that literature will never replace politics. That their importance and effects are so unequal is self evident. When a book fails the only people to lose are the publisher and author; when a bad policy fails everyone suffers the consequences.

In the face of such manifest incapacity, one is necessarily led to ask how it is that literature has throughout history attracted the attention of the powerful in this world. One must similarly ask how it has managed to attract so much suspicion and mistrust and why so much of its history is the history of persecution. Does literature have more influence than it would want to admit? If one starts from the principle that literature is useless, how does one explain the unceasing efforts of the powerful to obtain the services of writers and make them elegant mouthpieces of their masters' voice, whose single refrain is 'the country is at peace'? The goal has often been to make the writer a backstairs merchant of the imaginary, an organizer of the unreal. He is to be tolerated like the ornamental fish trapped inside an aquarium. The mere fact that literature has been so constantly viewed with suspicion or contempt is evidence enough.

Literature changes our view of the world

It is obvious that suspicion and contempt are not comparable with the idea that literature is utterly without influence. Are such reactions thus to be judged as pointless? The answer is yes—but also, and emphatically, no. Vigilance has always been justified; for even if literature has not succeeded in offering a total solution to the most dramatic problem of a period, in providing the necessary stimulus to resolve the needs of the moment and to enthrone reason in majority, it is not without influence. Though literature has been unable to transform situations, it has succeeded in changing our relationship to the world. This it has done through analysis, the heightening of consciousness, and the unveiling of reality. By offering alternative solutions, it has obliged mankind to ponder its own situation and to face up to the reality of its condition. Though often acting defensively, literature has ensured that the dream of a better world shall not be abandoned. In a message that is by definition addressed to the individual, it ceaselessly invites him to compare his destiny with that of others and, when necessary, to draw conclusions from that comparison. It is precisely this uncontrollable dialogue with the individual that gives rise to such suspicion and distrust and explains why the powerful view literature as a subversive threat. Literature has, furthermore, always been a means of preserving the past and has always presented itself as a limitless repository of memory. Simply to entrench memory can already represent a form of resistance, at least in circumstances when to forget becomes desirable—or even obligatory.

Must literature challenge? The answer is yes and it could never be otherwise since the reality which it has faced allows for no other solution. Its oppositionism obviously resides in the fact that it offers a challenge to an order created by violence, that it refuses an imposed silence and speaks for those who have been reduced to silence. Going on the attack in order to serve a better peace—a peace that is not phoney—literature also reminds us that the past does not stop; by participating in man's nature and role it also challenges the present. Thus it is clear that without this challenge the peace which we will never cease to seek can never be attained.

We cannot be content with a definition of peace as the absence of war. Even definitions grow old, inadequate and threadbare and cease to reflect the transformations that an idea will undergo. Observe, for example, the profound and significant difficulties involved in the attempt to define the concept of violence: for Kant, one of its most bitter critics, the reference is clearly to a higher order whereas for Alfred Grosser, from the perspective of our own time, a whole range of factors is involved. Just as the definition of violence must be considered from a broader perspective, so must we broaden our definition of 'peace' and, at the very least, ask ourselves if peace breaks out when the noise of battle stops. We are entitled to think—and experience tells us—that our carefully considered refusal of war does not thereby guarantee a pacific approach to our social, or private, life or to the problems of our age. I do not know whether we are entitled to hope that we will ever become pacific; but the painful inadequacy of the peace in which we find ourselves would seem to confirm my doubts. These doubts grow ever deeper justified by situations which do not allow one to talk of true peace but at best of an incomplete one. Let us now look at this notion of what else should be involved in a peace beyond armistices, pacts and treaties.

Bitter but unsurprised

It did not need Shakespeare's kingship dramas to tell us the things that power conceived of and was ready to do to preserve itself—classical antiquity already provided plenty of examples. The ancient world showed not only that there was a sense of practical methods to eliminate dissidents and rivals—those who corrupted youth and the enemies of the state—but also that words themselves carry their own dangers. Once uttered and repeated they become a weapon and a threat; they contain demands, as in the classic demand for bread, justice, and liberty, and they can call into question the autonomy that power has created for itself. Sadly, experience is not limited to the ancient world. The threat which words can represent is shown by a report of the International Pen Club 'Writers in Prison'. It dates from 1988 and asserts that at that time 305 writers and journalists were incarcerated in countries with which we have economic and cultural, perhaps even friendly, links and to which we are bound by differing types of alliance. Because the rulers did not agree with the way that 305 men and women used words they threw them in prison. It is true that the total is slightly lower than that for a year earlier. Nevertheless, the report stresses that this minor reduction in no way indicates that freedom of speech has evolved in the world in the way that one might hope. We all know the motives that have led to the arrests and charges; they are the old and repulsive motives which a mistrustful power uses to return to silence those who might challenge the prevailing silence of the grave in their countries.

At once bitter and unsurprised, we learn that a woman poet has been condemned for evoking in her verse a massacre which her government had committed: it is illegal to recall the memory of a day of national shame. It is clear that what is found reprehensible is the possible incitement to revolt. Another is condemned for talking with some students about poems which glorified the ideals of democracy; and a third because he had actually written a 'book of democracy'.

As I analyse the charges made against them I am not surprised to find that the most frequent crime is that of 'plotting against the State'. The words are alleged to reveal a 'revolt against the authorities'; they are provocations against heads of state; they propagate subversive thoughts and are hence counter revolutionary; they diffuse among the population a 'dangerous ideology'; and they distort the statements of members of government and thus threaten peace. On the nature of this kind of peace there is little to be said; as the *Writers in Prison* report shows, punishment can follow someone who propagates Marxist ideas just as it can someone who refused to accept the catechism of Marxist ideas.

Whatever peace among men is, it is not palms and cymbals. Nor is it man's essential goodness and self-sacrificing happiness. Peace of the sort that we seek will include tension, conflict and the inevitability of disturbance. The more peace allows for our contradictions, the stronger it will be. And this is why we cannot be satisfied with a peace in which there is no conflict, no challenge or opposition to the existing state of affairs. Even if the holders of power believe that they are entitled to think and speak in our name, the happiness promised to all of us on the planet will not exist so long as freedom of expression is not guaranteed for all. Such freedom is part of peace, one of its defining elements and a fundamental demand.

As a demand, it is also a very old one, and one that we must make our own, in the same way that we must remind the world of what the ancient prophets saw as indispensable for peace. That which has been prevented from being heard for two thousand years is not thereby archaic: to bury hatred and give up the sword, put an end to tyranny and create a state in which, as Amos said, right flows like water and justice like a flood; are demands which, though ancient, conserve their value today. It is true that the great gospels often depend on that little word 'when' ('when governments shall have become wise and wolves vegetarian')—but this does not prevent the ancient prophets from being amongst the greatest spirits of enlightenment. They showed us that external and internal peace cannot be separated, that external peace finds its complement and its echo in internal peace.

A long term objective that is utopian yet necessary

What is internal peace? Perhaps it is that 'full presence of self' of which Ernest Bloch spoke. Perhaps it is the end of a long quest for identity, the 'happy ending' of a painful search for oneself: union with oneself and with the world. Perhaps one can find internal peace in the smile of contentment, or in the satisfaction that a person can derive from their work. Once our hopes are achieved we abandon ourselves to the belief that we have done all that could be done—nothing is left unfinished, all aspirations have been realized and perfect harmony rules. I believe that internal peace will always remain a long term objective (but an objective that is none the less vital) and one that, even if we were to arrive at it, would remain more difficult to realize than external peace since it is not, as the world knows, man's natural conditon.

But we should remind ourselves also of another dimension of peace. I understand perfectly why armaments conflict has such an extraordinary importance for our lives, I am fully aware that the mastery of conflict depends upon disarmament and the installation of a European security system; yet even if these problems could be resolved in a satisfactory manner, it certainly does not follow that a satisfactory peace would ensue.

For there is more to peace than the explicit renunciation of violence. Peace means a state in which all have the right to hope and all share responsibility for what is and what has been. Hans Jonas defines responsibility as the charge of something which has been given to us. That something might be new neighbours, a weakling, a lost sheep; it might also be knowledge, the water by which we live, or our own history. And we must take responsibility for that which we are given, however difficult it may be.

We recently witnessed a controversy on the history of Germany which is known as the 'Historian's quarrel' and attracted world-wide attention. We watched with horror as university academics attempted to deny the consequences of Auschwitz—the industrialized murder of millions of human beings—and thus to render it 'understandable'. By referring to Stalin's Gulag

Archipelago, in which millions had already died, these academics sought to make us believe that this was where Hitler got his example. To put it bluntly, we were asked to accept the following principle: 'There would have been no Auschwitz without the Gulag'. And after this devastating conclusion we were taught that it was time to historicize the Third Reich, to 'dedramatize' its work and its crimes. Historicization and dedramatization were invoked as the way to arrive at a final explanation of historical events. But history is not only about explaining the past; it is also about informing the present. Does history really talk to us? Does it say anything to us if we approach it without any passion, and observe with imperturbable detachment the passage of events? And what type of understanding will it offer us, if we are so neutralized by it that we give a scientific account of an unspeakable horror? I cannot bring myself to believe that detachment is a historians' virtue. If 'historicization' means considering an event as a completed, finished, and terminated sequence, from which all the horror has been purged, then it is a strange form of historical knowledge. For history is never ended, it always spills over into the present, it always conveys something and always disconcerts, it forces us to remember, traps us and makes us shudder at the thought of what man is capable. To understand the spirit—or the madness—of a period, what is needed is not so much dedramatization as judgemental participation, for the cause of mankind is always involved.

Anyone can discover a historical document but only those who do not dehumanize themselves can uncover the spirit of an age. Other people's crimes do not absolve us of responsibility. Auschwitz cannot be explained by reference to an historical parallel that will result, whether deliberately or not, in the minimization of its importance. And Auschwitz in any case passes understanding. Obviously we should always try to understand before we judge; but a crime like Auschwitz reveals the limits of understanding. And I wonder how its victims and its survivors, those who are still among us, would react to our need to understand. Dolf Sternberger has said all that needs to be said on this subject: 'If science really is nothing more than the desire to understand then the only possible conclusion is that science is incapable of understanding the phenomenon of Auschwitz'.

However bizarre it may seem, Auschwitz remains our responsibility. Auschwitz belongs to us, just as the rest of our own history belongs to us. We cannot live at peace with that history, for its implications and its challenges are endless. In the circumstances, it is not the intellectual inheritance of Hegel's universal spirit that is in question but the unbearable sufferings whose memory we have inherited. Thus one must ask if it is possible to imagine a peace which has space for the unendurable. I believe that we can. The peace which we desire does not exclude the disturbance of memory. Though we cannot be reconciled with our past, we are, for that reason, even more passionate in our support for peace. We give to the past that which we owe it and to the present that which makes it bearable. As the President of West Germany, Richard Weizsacker has said, 'To close ones eyes to the past makes one blind to the present'.

A glut of information

We can see clearly that history has no final goal and is not moving towards some brilliant apotheosis. As it moves on, it shrugs its shoulders at our actions, our errors and our misfortunes, we can have little confidence in the lessons it provides so lavishly. Gandhi's assessment of his long life seems irrefutable: 'History teaches man that history teaches man nothing'. Yet there is something that we can learn: that each age has its own demands and that we cannot do other than respond to them. This also is part of our work in favour of peace.

Whenever events occur today, we are informed. As soon as something breaks up, or the powerful make war on their own people, or a plague of locusts occurs, or some dolphins come to the aid of the navy, or treaties are signed and politicians fall into each others arms, we know and we cannot avoid knowing. And virtually every day we learn about misery: misery in the slums of the starving countries, misery in the desert regions. We think that we know about everything. Glutted with information, we tell ourselves that the world has become smaller. And such is indeed the case. We are fully entitled to wonder what else this old and battered planet can still bear and endure. In the face of the demographic explosion, and even supposing that we have enough to eat and are warm, how many of us can have any hopes of life or peace.

Given the finite nature of natural resources and the speed with which the worlds' population has tripled, I do not think we can exclude the probability that peace will be threatened by what Lenin—and, be it said, others—called 'just wars'. This faces us all with an unavoidable problem. How *can* a war appear just, or inevitable, or even holy, when one knows in advance that it will cause so many deaths? No cause can justify the violent death of our fellow men, not even the grand designs which the powerful summon up when Reason disappears. Yet if we are to take into account—as we must—the possibility of one of these 'just' wars, we must show our concern in time, that is to say, at once. In order to resist the source of conflict which is social misery, a misery that affects thousands of millions of future people, we must start to act today.

When I was born, there were two thousand million human beings on the planet; today there are five thousand million and the statistics of the American Population Office forecast six thousand million for the end of the century. It can be taken as certain that thousands of millions of the coming generation will not be able to count even on the meagre satisfaction that work brings to life. Yet they will be no less obliged to eat. Given that even today millions of people are dying of hunger, what are the new food resources that must be developed to prevent them dying in their thousands of millions? Such questions are not likely to put our consciences at rest. We will not win the peace unless we are prepared to take responsibility for the misery of the Third World, both its present misery and its future, yet more terrible, misery. It is clear that a new social and economic organization of international dimensions would help to reduce the misery. But it seems to me equally important that we should also establish a plan of action for the demographic policy that is indispensable if we are to live together in harmony on this small planet.

All the experts agree that the demographic crisis is the consequence, and not the cause, of under-development. Any solution for such problems faces a whole series of obstacles. One of the most difficult problems is religious belief. It is obvious that wherever birth control and family planning appear, the inevitable means of controlling the demographic explosion, such measures come into conflict with the dictates of religion. And the latter forms part of our culture. They determine our conception of married and family life and organize our daily life at the same time as they confirm the necessity of a spiritual universe. The contradiction is thus evident. How could a population policy be established that would not lead to the eradication of belief and religious values or at the very least to a reduction in their influence on the way we live?

We know that religious principles can be interpreted in different ways and that some parts of the Koran give rise to astonishingly varied readings; but no possible reinterpretation of those norms and values can form the basis of a global programme. The crucial element is the agreement of all the heads of state of all the governments in the world. With his typical sense of the demands of the present, Helmut Schmidt assembled political and religious leaders for a conference on the problems of peace and world population. Islamics, Christians, Jews, Hindus, and Buddhists came together and, as one might expect, all agreed that the evolution of the world's population is one of the most pressing problems of our age. But agreement and understanding are not enough; we need a new policy, a policy which takes account of these initial conclusions and agreements, a properly universal policy. And we need it straightaway since its effects—as can be calculated—will not be felt for several decades. The will for peace resides here; it is with this problem that one can see it at work.

Violence and threats are part of the present state of peace

Thus we can see that for a whole series of reasons the peace we live is imperfect and limited. If one followed the example of politicians, economists, and commentators one would be tempted to bring it before some sort of supreme court, so that a legal definition might be given of peace, its assumptions and achievements. I assume that a trial of this sort would confront, analyse, compare, and judge the different faces of war and different forms of peace with all the intellectual rigour and all the matchless linguistic precision that a supreme court should have. I would not envy the position of the judges: it is difficult to see how they would not be immediately obliged to acknowledge that certain defining criteria of law—for example, violence and threats—can equally be found in the peace we experience today. And would they not be also forced to recognize that what we allow to occur in time of peace—the poisoning of the soil, the pollution of water, the numberless silent deaths of animals and plants—are effectively acts of war? Our age no longer allows for the clear definition of concepts. Even the language of militant pacifism resorts to the terminology of war and employs notions like strategy, potential, blockade.

We live in a state of peace and yet are exposed to violence, a violence that has its privileges, is blessed by public authority and makes our world ever more uninhabitable. Against our will, we are deprived of our lakes and our seas; our water-springs are destroyed and our forests are reduced to skeletons. A court has declared that voices raised to protest against such events are morally defendable but juridically illegal. So this is the state we have reached: to wish to remain loyal to creation can be an illegal act. One is indeed entitled to ponder the nature of laws which allow violence to be employed against those who do not profit from the destruction of the environment. It is sadly true, as disillusioned politicians have acknowledged, that the influence of the economy is much greater than that of politics.

Just as our present state of peace manifests violence, it also contains other elements which threaten it. Such threats are wide ranging. The Toronto conference on world climatic conditions reached the conclusion that the dangers which our atmosphere faces are comparable with those of an atomic war. The greenhouse effect created by the atmospheric accumulations of industry and agriculture may have catastrophic consequences for life on earth. The warming of the planet will increase the number of deserts, melt the polar regions, lead to a raising of sea levels which in turn will drown entire countries. If industry and agriculture continue to develop as they have done up until now, this disastrous warming could occur in barely fifty years. The scientific terminology for this is of 'a major extra-military threat against international security'. The first signs of the catastrophe are already visible: unusually long periods of drought and floating masses of deadly seaweed. In my judgement the extinction of life has become a possibility.

Creation dies slowly. It is not necessarily doomed to disappear in an atomic explosion which would boil the oceans and melt down the mountains. It could quite simply die from our indifference and our selfishness. The appeals we hear from all sides are useless, we know how powerless and ineffective they are.

If there is any way of changing the course of future development, it can only be an energetic and resolute policy to win back the zones of action that have been lost to the economy and to industry. We have no ticket to eternity and it doesn't take much imagination to visualize an uninhabited world, one covered in a dust that swirls around under freezing winds. As a memorial to our age we could write on its tombstone: everyone wanted to do their best—for themselves.

We live at peace, but a peace that is imperfect, indigent and always under threat. Given the forces that oppose peace, the costs that it has to bear and the tasks which it imposes upon us, we can conclude by saying that if peace is to be served we must resist all those who through their desire for power, their selfishness, and an absence of morality in the management of their affairs, threaten its very existence.

Book Reviews

Book Reviews

The Memory's Silence

*Jacques Tarnero**

Never was the spirit of the time as retrospective as it was in 1989. The French Bicentenary has made it so, without us really knowing whether its memory is being faithfully confirmed. It is strange when the commemoration of events contributes to the confusion of history, to its misdirection. It is almost as if the present, in a world devoid of hope, needs to align history's origins with its own construction of them in order to uphold some virtue and to prove its faithfulness to a founding myth. In a present without ideological causes but full of show, the relentless intellectual debate about the past seems both derisory and unavoidable. The Heidegger affair and the Heidegger 'effect', German arguments over their responsibility for the Second World War, the Waldheim issue in Austria, French revisionism from Faurisson to Roques, including Le Pen's claim that the gas chambers were but a 'detail' of the 1939–1945 period; decidedly, today's intellectual debate is not forward looking, and the current Carmel of Auschwitz affair with the controversies or misunderstandings that it is creating in Europe at the time of the Polish upheaval reveals the weight of a past which is always present. It is a derisory debate because all the signs are that the media's necrophilia has submerged the need to understand the past. It is an unavoidable debate precisely because the past's ghosts are returning before we have been able to devise a version of history which excludes them. What sort of consensus comes

* Jacques Ternero is a sociologist. He is reviewing here Nicole Lapierre's *Le silence de la mémoire* (Paris: Plon, 1989).

from forgetting? What sort of reconstruction of French history comes from supressing the memory of the Algerian war? For what sort of European vision is the single market of 1992 being established? Is forgetting the past the necessary price of future unity?

Between the showy version of the past and the forgetting of it, there are, fortunately, those killjoys who are attached to the accurate portrayal of the past, the relentless upholders of the memory of the past, who are all the more relentless because they are trying to prevent its collective memory from being erased. And it is just this erasure of the collective memory which is threatened today: erasure by substitution, by revision, by negation, by misrepresentation, by disappearance. Will there still be enough historians to tell the story one day of history's deletions? Nicole Lapierre is one of those working against this erasure. She is putting ink back on the page where the pen had dried up. Her *Le silence de la mémoire* (*The Memory's Silence*) is both a personal quest and the scientific work of a historian, ethnographer, and sociologist. This research about the Jews from Plock in Poland is not one of these heroic family sagas which constitute the publishers' successful Jewish market. The approach is sober to match the silence which has surrounded Polish Judaism since 1945. Inheritor or trustee of a story which dared not be told, Nicole Lapierre wanted to find, to understand, the hidden past of the Polish Jews through her own piece of history, that of the immediate post-war generation. This confrontation which explains her reasons for the research also gives the book its tone and style: respectful and detailed. There is no exhibitionism in this writing only the regaining of her origins and a fidelity to her past which was once obfuscated in the same way as her name when it was changed from 'Lipsztein' to 'Lapierre'. The change of identity did not efface her past, quite the contrary; it appears to have stimulated her research. In the description of her name change Nicole Lapierre depicts a delightful incident. What surprises the Jews originating from Plock whom she interviewed was that a Lapierre should question them. They ask her 'the French National Council for Scientific

Research, is it a Jewish organisation?', but quickly add, 'Ah! Your father is from Plock'. So the story can be told. It is conveyed in an intimate, sensitive and involved way.

Nicole Lapierre has gone back through the history of the Jews in Poland, a history which was finally reduced to dust. She links together the major events: the 'lost time' of the large communities thrown from transitory splendour to pogroms, the 'countdown of time' which marks the fleeing and wandering, the 'pulverised time' which saw the beings and buildings which were left transformed to ashes and dust, and finally the 'refound time' in which the remains of the past are collected together and brought into the present. Nicole Lapierre has managed to put in order the survivors' stories which seem to fill this black hole of Europe's memory. Through laborious archival work and textual archeology in the style of those who discovered the Qumram manuscripts in bottles by the Dead Sea the author takes up the written accounts found in a bottle hidden in 1942. It is the first account of the Jewish community in Plock to its last breath of life. Through the meandering tales, the shreds and the remaining traces of the hundred accounts collected, she weaves this story. But this book is much more than a work of ethnological research. Nicole Lapierre invites us to reflect on the relationships of time, of memory, of history, of mourning, and of the transmission of history. Her journey is the opposite to forgetting, through the words of the survivors she is encouraging the world to hold out against the forces of amnesia.

A Europe of Regions: the Example of Andalusia

Sami Nair

Tomorrow's Europe will not be simply a Europe of nations, but a Europe of regions. We shall see developing at the politico-cultural level a phenomenon that Europe has already known in its past: whole regions will reorientate themselves into zones which transcend the central authority of the state. Eastern France will look towards Germany, French and Spanish Catalonia will elaborate joint ventures, Spain and Portugal, across their frontier divisions, will reawaken their ancestral relationship. A new kind of territoriality is very slowly developing. The twenty-first century will see many examples of regional osmosis and, inevitably, the emergence of new forms of cultural relations. Today there is little preparing us mentally for such polycentric developments, but the economy itself is already responding to the changes. Already new economic relations have been established which will create irreversible shifts. In order to ensure and control this economic and cultural change, we need to understand the state of the regions today.

In terms of offering such understanding, Danielle Provansal and Pedro Molina's excellent book *Campo de Nijar*[1] is exemplary. It is not a dry book where statistics compete with diagrams—and often mask a lack of sensitivity to the subject matter. On the contrary, this is a study which brings together developmentally an anthropology of lived experiences, which

---

[1] Danielle Provansal and Pedro Molina, *Campo de Nijar: cortijeros y areneros* (Instituto de Estudios Almerienses, Almería, 1989).

reconstructs deep mental structures of self-identity through a judicious use of people's personal recollections with a systematic and rigorous analysis of the economic processes experienced by the Campos de Nijar region, near Almería in Spain. The study is all the more welcome because, traditionally and for many reasons, this part of Andalusia has rarely interested researchers. The particular character of Southern Andalusia is little known, even by many of its own inhabitants who still—though this is becoming more and more criticized—adopt an 'acultural' attitude (no stress upon origins, ignorance of specific cultural traits, and so on), while in the rest of Spain cultural assertions and clashes are increasing. The book aims, therefore, to make the population aware of its own singular nature, both by rediscovering its history and through a unique reading of the countryside and of the changes wrought in it over the last twenty years.

The Campos de Nijar is a desert which men and women have tried to molify and master. Already at the end of the 1950s Juan Goytisolo had revealed this region to the world through his famous book, *Campos de Nijar*. What he revealed was a kind of Africa, a kind of desert inside a European country, a place where the rural exodus seemed to be the only response to the increasing drought conditions in the area. Provansal and Molina's book is an attempt, echoing the literary sensitivity of the earlier writer, to describe the various developmental strategies elaborated by the people living there to avoid disappearing along with their region. The authors show with discernment how these economic strategies were elaborated by peasant families across time, subtly combining local resources, extracted with great pain from excessively fragmented lands (minifundia on the one hand, absentee latifundia on the other), with outside trade made possible by numerous other complementary activities. However, instead of falling into the trap of classic 'anthropologism' which places emphasis upon traditional aspects which artificially construct an industrious and secular peasant world, Danielle Provansal and Pedro Molina demonstrate, on the contrary, the modernity of peasant behaviour and the fragility of economic interrelationships caused by an increase in property concentration. There are also a great deal of illuminating analyses on the economic and social changes which, at different times, have shaped the strategies of local groups and, in the course of recent decades, given new techniques such as cultivation on sand, and under glass, have metamorphosed the countryside, the human habitat, and the organization of agricultural work. The authors show, moreover, that the continuing existence of family farms, and the use of domestic labour, are integrated in a network of widened dependence which has an international aspect to it. Hence the changes in the relationship to the land itself (where private property has less and less meaning), and a situation where traditional ties of solidarity and mutual assistance create new relations of subordination and new systems of organization. Also of interest is the examination of agricultural policy under Franco, an under-researched area as far as this region is concerned. The authors show how, via particular strategies, the logic of the market breaks and then reorientates traditional relationships. They also are at pains, however, to see this development within the historico-cultural context of the whole region, a historical context which includes both slavery and the expulsion of the Moors at the beginning of the seventeenth century. This region was, in fact, one of the last bastions of the Moors who combated the Christians and helped the Barbary pirates. Facts such as these are engraved in the collective memory of the inhabitants of the *campos*, and it is to Provansal and Molina's credit that they not only bring out these deep themes but also show their function in the creation of a regional identity. It is through these themes too that we sense the reality and significance of a wider Mediterranean culture borne of human intermixing and interrelation across mountains and the sea.

This is indeed a remarkable book which heralds the reconquest of regional identities within the wider European context.

The Cinematographic East: a Heritage for Tomorrow

*Alain Bellet**

Having applauded Miklos Jancso's films (*Red Psalm* [*Még kér a nép*], *Red and White* [*Csillagosok Katonak*], *For Electra* [*Elektra*]), viewed and re-viewed at least ten times Eisenstein's *Potemkin*, *October*, or *The Strike*, Westerners reckon they know the cinema of the Eastern bloc. How wrong they are.

From time to time they stumble over a 'new' filmmaker and he becomes all the rage. Ever since *glasnost*'s partial lifting of censorship, cinephiles discovered, two years ago, Kira Muratovà's films (*Brief Encounters* [*Korotkie Vstreci*], *Long Goodbyes* [*Dolgie provody*], *Our Honest Bread* [*Nach Tchestniy Khaleb*]) which are a true Soviet equivalent to the French New Wave of the 1960s. Or again, amongst their discoveries, they have found films of Georgian filmmakers, like Lana Gogoberidze (*The Whirlwind* [*Krougovorod*]), who are authors of genuine oxygen balloons in the bureaucratic, centralized world of hieratic Russia. How many are they today to emerge from the shadows, hitting us with their poetic intensity, their astounding humanism, their vengeful gaze on their collective history?

Censorship is lifted, but it leaves behind it the dust gathered on the metallic boxes that fill the shelves with commissioned work which had been unjustifiably rendered obsolete. This directly or indirectly commissioned cinema, realistic or justifi-

* Alain Bellet is a film critic and novelist. Here he reviews *Le Cinéma de l'Est* (*The Cinema of the Eastern Bloc*) by Antonin and Mira Liehm, published by Editions du Cerf in the collection 7ᵉArt, 1989.

catory of political practices, represents an unexplored mass and, amongst these obsolete fossils, hundreds of masterpieces unknown to the West.

A renewal

For several years now, Yugoslavia, Hungary, and to a smaller extent Czechoslovakia, have given the world's cinema a new lease of life—in particular to the *auteur* cinema. Everywhere filmmakers are standing up and being counted, bespeaking a general thaw. As early as the end of the 1970s, Wadja was imposing a critical eye on Polish society (*The Man of Marble, The Man of Iron*). In 1981, Istvan Szabo, with his film *Mephisto*, opened the debate on the artist sold to the totalitarian state. The target was nazism, but the lesson was intended to go further.

All these movements heralding an opening out, a thaw, *glasnost*, question again the relations between these peoples trying to break the bureaucratic yokes and the Eastern bloc cinema production. The moment was ripe, therefore, for a text of reference.

A remarkable piece of work

Mira and Antonin Liehm's book *Le Cinéma de l'Est* is the first book to make an inventory of all the filmic productions. In their analyses of films, country by country, period by period, they break new ground in their efforts to show how the cinema of the Eastern bloc reflects the political stakes at play, the ebb and flow of mass movements, the democratic opening up of the political spectrum or, conversely, the bureaucratic clamp-downs dictated by the stalinist machinery.

The pre-war period: a timely reminder

The book begins with an overview of the origins of the cinemas of central Europe and the Eastern bloc and brings out, quite perceptively, their strong distinctivenesses according to their respective countries, to the conceptions of art in force, and to the importance in the different states of the literary, theatrical or plastic art movements.

The cinema is 'the most important art form', said Lenin whilst in full civil war. And up until the Second World War, it was to undergo a number of varied treatments. However, whether a major or a marginal production, it questioned social movements, the authorities, and artistic avant-gardes.

From the Polish cinema joining up with the left-wing artists of the 'City Suburbs' group, to the Czech cinema—the hub of Central Europe's avant-gardes—the cinematograph and its first theoreticians were already situating all questions related to creation within the context of politics, the masses, the cultural evolution of a nation and its peoples. In 1918, Hungary national-ized film production, a few months later Lenin signed the decrees ordering the second nationalization of cinema in history.

October, and then Stalin

In the emerging Soviet nation, cinema was very quickly perceived to be a marvellous instrument for educating the masses, all to the purpose of successfully building the Soviet states. Wherever backwardness or illiteracy still prevailed, cine-matographic production, as with the theatre, was given a clear propagandistic mission. The artists 'saved cinema from the claws of capitalism', and worked towards the transformation 'of a product of consumption exclusively conceived for profit into an art sustained by society'. Heady on the rapture of the revolution, the films of Eisenstein, Pudovkin (*The Mother*), Kulechov and Vertov were all part of the liberating sloganeering and the cele-bration of the workers' and peasants' newly acquired dignity. In their book, the authors stress that 'The Soviet cinema in its infancy was discovering a new language . . . through their experimenting with editing techniques (e.g. *montage*), their new ideas on scenarios and new documentary techniques, the young Soviet filmmakers had carved themselves a place in cinema's history'.

However, in the event, the internal struggles of the Soviet revolution and Stalin's victory over the old-guard Bolsheviks culminated in depriving the cinema of its artistic value and creative independence. Henceforth cinema would be about 'the nuts and bolts' of socialist realism promoted by Stalin and theorized in Jdanov's infernal doctrinaire writings. Compliance was obligatory.

Mira and Antonin Liehm recall the struggles of the Russian filmmakers against bureaucracy, their fights, their self-doubts, their tragic endings like Meyerhold's who was tortured after a courageous intervention: 'Along with hope, talent has disappeared . . . in your efforts to eradicate formalism you have killed art!'

Eisenstein ceased making films and Soviet cinema 'slumped into a state of stagnation at the very moment when it should have been mobilizing the masses faced with the threat of war'. The production of that period proves that 'buoyant commissioning, official aesthetics and police control beget artistic impotence'. The authors' indictment is severe. It shows how the Stalin régime shattered cinematographic art, leaving in our Western memory only the major works created before the invasion of the sound-track. That is to say, before the liquidation of the opposition of the left, and some years before the Moscow trials.

A process of politico-artistic thought

Through a systematic analysis the book uncovers with precision the advances or set-backs of cinematographic creation, country by country, since the Second World War; and it does so by pointing to the dialectical relationships between cinema and the different political periods from the point of view of the evolution or degradation of democracy.

The authors explain how the Soviet Union swopped the tastes of the real spectators for those of the 'exceptional spectator', for it was Stalin who laid down the guide lines that cinema was to follow . . .

The death of the Little Father of the People and the process of destalinization started at the XXI Congress of the CPSU unfortunately did not bring about the disappearance of Jdavonist theories which had completely clamped down on cinema and artistic practices. With socialist realism surviving its Master, the cinema remained henceforth a state matter, a matter for the Soviet States. From 1945 to 1955, the cinemas of Eastern Europe virulently attack cosmopolitanism, bourgeois objectivism, and denounce submission to the West. A scarcely hidden anti-semitism is silhouetted in a number of official films. 'The writer, the artist is no longer just the engineer of the soul, now he is expected to be a soldier submitted to obedience whose task it is to ensure that others—the spectators—are similarly obedient.' In its narration of the battle of Stalingrad, *The Turning Point* [*Veliki perelom*] corresponded to the State's discourse—'the struggle between two generations, the one that lost the war and the one that won it'—even so, its director, Ermier, gave evidence of a genuine artistic revival.

The pioneers of a new cinema

Any attenuation of the ideological yoke and the various interdicts—whether in Hungary, Czechoslovakia, or Poland—is, the authors remind us, in direct proportion to the extent of the political thaw and the efforts towards democratization. In Poland, Jerzy Kawalerowicz' films (*The Village Mill* [*Gromada*], *A Night of Memories* [*Celuloza*], *Under the Phrygian Star* [*Pod gwiazda frygiska*]) topple the reigning academicism, abandon the pre-established image constructions, examine thoroughly the 'allegory of intolerance that destroys both its inquisitors and their victims'. Munk, Ford, and Wadja continue their own particular trajectory. Films produced in the Soviet Union over this same period, however, remain uncluttered with historic reality, rather they glorify history in motion—thus Stalin becomes the hero of the October revolution in Ermier's *The Unforgettable Year 1919* and in Loukov's *The Miners of Dombass* gives a flattering portrait of the quinquennial plans that glosses over the reality of the workings of the Soviet administration.

In the Democratic Republic of Germany, current theory addresses 'love under the socialist regime, for a film cannot content itself with being a love story pure and simple if it claims to be a realist film, love cannot be abstracted from social considerations . . .'

In Czechoslovakia, the style of the new realism is directly correlated to the purges and trials (Slansky in 1952): to escape dictats and multiple censorship, Trnka and Zeman developed animated film and thus created truly poetic works which were free from directives.

During the 1950s and 1960s, the bloody suppressions which hit first Hungary and then Czechoslovakia stopped the momentum for a new cinema. Numerous filmmakers chose to emigrate to the West; directors such as Roman Polanski, Milos Forman, Andrei Konchalovski, Iosseliani, and later on Skolimwski and Tarkovski.

The art of the possible

Other filmmakers preferred to stay, thus providing their respective countries with beautiful masterpieces. The Czechoslovak, Vera Chytilova (*The Daisies* [*Sedmitasky*]), 'in comparing success with failure, introduced a philosophical dimension unheard of till now'. The normalization that followed the Prague Spring put an end to the blossoming of a Czech art cinema forcing numerous filmmakers to emigrate. In Poland, Has and Wadja continued to develop an inventive cinema. In the USSR Larissa Chepitko (*The Horses of Fire* [*Teni zabytykh predkov*], *The Legend of the Fortress of Souram* [*Leguenda o souramskoï Kreposti*]) tackled the major themes of sacrifice and treachery. However, the greatest Soviet filmmaker, Paradjenov, was condemned to long sentences of deportation.

Little by little, within and without the borders of the Eastern bloc, the art of the possible imposed itself. Several films won international prizes, most notably at Cannes (Mikhalkov's *Black Eyes* [*Oci ciorne*]). The cinema of the Soviet republics acquired a greater status thanks to such films as *Repent* [*Pokaianie*] by